In Your Heart

The key to Astonishing Performance

Ian Hunter
Chris Stock

First published 2012

by In Your Heart Ltd.

Albany House, 63 Albany Road, Old Windsor, Berkshire,
SL4 2QD

© 2012 In Your Heart Ltd.

Cover Design by Anita Capewell

ISBN 978-0-9574506-2-2

Preface

About this book

The idea for this book was born when two professional chaps decided one day to do something a little different, in fact to tackle a huge challenge: to cycle through the Himalayas. No ordinary mountain-biking for them, but an experience that would require them to train for months to reach the appropriate level of fitness, to take on a terrain that would certainly provide a number of steep ups and downs. And for Ian, there was a spiritual dimension too: his good friend Andy Lee had recently died, and Ian wanted to do something in his memory. He decided that his journey to the Himalayas would culminate in a visit to the home of the Dalai Lama, where he would leave Andy's order of funeral service. For Chris, the less fit of the two men, being able to enjoy the trip and appreciate the surroundings without absolute exhaustion setting in was his goal.

Acknowledgements

The authors would like to thank all our friends and families for their help and support in putting this together, especially Lisa, James and Rebecca for their ongoing tolerance, and Pat and Harry. Thanks to Paul Slyfield for all his help and Callum Harvey for organising us on the first phase of the book. Special thanks to Lyn, without whose support and patience this book would not have been finished.

In particular they would like to thank the Pujari at the Lakewale temple whose words inspired the creation and focus of the book.

Introduction

"The only way to do great work is to love what you do. If you haven't found it yet, keep looking. Don't settle. As with all matters of the heart, you'll know when you find it."
Steve Jobs

This book is a modern day handbook for astonishing performance. Unlike the majority of business books, it does not focus on form (how to do it); instead it focuses on the deeper and more human elements of becoming successful.

The inspiration for the book came during a cycling adventure through the Himalayas in India, where a Holy man shared his belief that the secret to achieving what we have been selected to do in life is in the HEART.

The authors have considered this proposition and developed a modern day approach to help understand what it takes to deliver astonishing performance: summarised by HEART as an acronym for Health; Energy; Authenticity; Resilience and Team.

HEART plays to the needs of people today for a greater connection to their personal spiritual and emotional selves and shows how a connection with these elements can lead to astonishing performance.

In developing the thinking of the HEART approach to astonishing performance the authors surveyed a cross-section of successful business leaders and practitioners, all of whom are either achieving or have already achieved astonishing performance. Those who contributed included international businessmen **Sir Paul Judge** and **Philip Oliver**, business writer **Laurie Young**, iBAHN Managing Director **Graeme Powell**, global executive coach **Elaine Waller**, President and COO of Numerix **Steve O'Hanlon**, Managing Director of Arco **Thomas Martin**, founder of award-winning agency Earnest **Paul Hewerdine**, Chairman and CEO of Continuous Insight group **Peter Pastides,** and General Manager at 3M **Fergal Morris**. We've taken the insight from our contributors, conducted a thorough literature search and brought together the key academic theories underpinning the elements of HEART, and documented them in the second part of this book.

Each element of HEART is interdependent. That is, you cannot succeed if one of the elements is missing; HEART comprises five areas of success that must be approached simultaneously if you are to achieve your goals.

The authors hope you find the book enjoyable and that it helps you on your journey to personal success. They are already seeing great results from those who have embraced the approach and put in personal action plans to maximise their chances of success.

How to use this book

Section 1 of *In your HEART* is a true story, which exemplifies the elements of HEART in the context of a cycling adventure in the Himalayas, written to be an easy read but with a serious outcome.

You could read this part as a travelogue, peppered with the insights that Ian and Chris were discovering at each stage of their journey.

The second part explains each of the insights of HEART in detail. Section 2 overviews the insight summarising the management theory and the insights gained from the leading contemporary business leaders, interviewed for this book. The HEART model is available as a management development tool and for more information please visit our website at *Inyourheart.co.uk*

Table of Contents

Section 1

The journey through the Himalayas

Chapter 1 - Health

Let's do it

A little while ago, Ian and Chris did all the usual things that business people do: go to meetings, make plans, talk about what they intended to do, wanting to sound as smart as possible, and of course, taking advantage of as many good lunches as they could. As a result, they were slightly overweight.

One day, over a coffee, they were having a coaching meeting, where Chris was sharing his ideas for the future and planning out the next steps in the direction of his business over the next couple of years. For both personal and business reasons, he wanted to do something adventurous, that would be hard to achieve, but when successful would provide plenty of material for his upcoming public-speaking engagements. Ian's mind was in a different place: he wanted to do something special as an act of remembrance for his friend Andy. But the two motivations coalesced when Ian suggested: "I know, let's do something together that's physically challenging and that will mean we'll need to get fit, and will be tough. How about we cycle in the most challenging terrain there is, the Himalayas?"

Chris, though initially taken aback, considered the idea seriously: "You know, that might just be the right thing to do, let's do it." Ian added, "And if we have as our destination the home of the Dalai Lama, I feel that would be a wonderful spiritual tribute to Andy. I know it's not going to be easy, but all the more worthwhile to me."

Now, many people will sit in a café bar and have a conversation like this, part ways and do nothing about it. Chris and Ian were different. They didn't just talk about it; they put talk into action. They believed it was important to create momentum.

Making it happen

The first step was to find an organisation that would support the logistics of the trip in northern India. After many hours of scouring the internet, travel companies and finally in newspapers, Ian found a company that gave him what he was looking for. It was local to the region in India, knew the terrain, and was experienced in supporting hiking and trekking trips. After many email exchanges, the route was roughly worked out. Next step was for Ian and Chris to book their flights to India, which gave them a date to aim for, made their discussion a reality, and motivated them to get into better shape. They now had nine months before they would fly out to begin the adventure.

Getting into shape

Chris was a big guy who took little more exercise than the walk to his car parked outside his home and who certainly didn't cycle up real mountains. He knew he needed to get healthier and fitter, but he was always too busy. And in reality, not being as fit as he should have been meant he was easily tired. He knew he was in a vicious circle of unfitness, but he hadn't really been able to break it. He knew that a focussed period of physical fitness training was needed over the next ten months.

Ian did the occasional mountain-biking trip, but didn't feel that he was particularly fit. He also would need to start training seriously. To manage the Himalayas, they would have to be able to climb up to 3200 metres, and be accustomed to sitting on the bikes for many hours duration.

To kick-start the training Ian suggested they take a long weekend in the mountains of Snowdonia, where Mount Snowdon, the highest peak in Wales, is situated. A three-day expedition in the Welsh mountains would be the perfect start to their training for the Himalayas, he thought.

Biking around Bangor

Ian was stunned when Chris arrived to meet him for their trip, wearing his old jeans, and with his antiquated bike. The bike was his pride and joy: he'd bought it at the age of seventeen, and he had saved up for a year to buy it. Chris was equally stunned when he saw Ian's LYCRA® cycling shorts and twenty-one gear mountain bike. When they looked at one another they realised the gap between them. Chris did not have a single item of the correct clothing or equipment. Seeing Ian, he realised this was much more serious than he had thought. On seeing Chris, Ian realised that Chris had no idea of the enormity of their undertaking. In reality, neither of them really knew what they had let themselves in for. But they both knew that Chris had the more work to do.

They travelled to Bangor in Wales and the Lon Ogwen cycle trail, a disused railway line that ran from the coalmines on Mount Snowdon down to the docks in Bangor for loading coal onto boats. It's a gentle climb for ten miles up to Lake Ogwen. Ian and Chris set off, quickly at first up the cycle trail but as they progressed Chris's bike began to make alarming squeaking sounds, getting louder and more frequent as they went. After a couple of miles there was a loud "clonk" and the crank fell off Chris's bike. "Great start," thought Chris.

Fortunately, they hadn't yet left the signs of habitation behind them completely, and found they were near some light industrial workshops. They went off in search of an engineer with the necessary tools to repair the bike. They were in luck.

The journey continued with lots of pushing and resting until the end of the trail. In fact there was a lot of resting as Chris was so unfit. He was out of breath and his whole body ached, and this was just the start of the three-day expedition. Chris thought about the time a few years previously when he had been fitter, and had taken part in a 10 mile run on the south coast of England called the Great South Run. As he ran the first half-mile along the sea front, he passed three overweight women already walking. He overheard one say to the other, "I'm thinking that maybe we should have prepared for this." Chris had been training for months for that run. Now on this bike ride, Chris knew exactly how those women had felt. He realised he would have to make huge training efforts before he would be ready for the Himalayas.

On the second day Ian and Chris cycled from the town of Llanberis two thirds of the way up the side of Mount

Snowdon and along Telegraph Valley and down to the
Snowdon Ranger station, about fifteen miles in all and with
some serious climbing. Chris amazed Ian with his
enthusiasm on the descent, at one point losing control and
rolling head over heels with his bike as he came down the
hill. He flew through the air and was lucky to land in the
thick grass at the side of the track.

The last day of training involved a beach ride, taking in a
small lighthouse, picturesque cottages and a long fast cycle
along the beautiful sandy beaches of Anglesey island. With
the tide out the beaches were wide, open and spacious. The
sand was flat and smooth with rocky outcrops and flanked
by grassy sand dunes. Nothing untoward happened on
this terrain, but it most certainly did not reflect the
Himalayas.

Getting into even more shape

The trip to Wales made them realise that they needed to
step up their fitness programme, and that they had a lot of
work to do, with rigorous training ahead.

Each man had his own fitness regime. As well as playing
tennis, Ian started running in the evenings, and at least
twice a week he'd manage a lunchtime run from the office.
At weekends he spent time cycling the English coast-to-
coast cycle way with his son, and mountain biking in the
hills and peaks of northern England. He cycled through a
variety of terrains on scenic routes such as Macclesfield
Forest, Buxton, Castleton and Marple Lakes. He really
enjoyed the scenic routes.

Chris went out training on his bike at least three times per week, and aimed to cover more than ten miles at weekends. He cycled through the Bracknell forest in southern England, where there was a short but steep hill within the woods. While taking his dogs for a run Chris would cycle up the hill, turn around and roll down, to start again. He hated this hill, but knew he needed to practise on hill-work. The dogs must have thought it was all some very strange game.

Chris looks back: "Thinking of my first trips cycling in the forest, I only cycled wide and paved paths, and most of the routes avoided steep hills wherever possible. I was really focussing on distance and endurance, to get my stamina up. I was definitely improving, as my circuits started to feel too easy. I knew that I needed to cycle on more challenging terrain."

More hills were needed for Chris, so they decided to tackle a cycle route across Helvellyn, England's second highest mountain. It was now only a couple of months before they would be cycling in the Himalayas.

Hell on Helvellyn

Ian searched in mountain bike books and internet blogs to find a challenging route up and across Helvellyn, believing that if they could do this they could do anything. He found one route, but it meant staying in a hut overnight. He worked out that if they were to reverse the published route, they could stay in a town overnight, which had a few bars and restaurants. Much more appealing, so why not? There seemed no reason on paper why they should not reverse the route.

The trip turned out to be a nightmare in so many ways. The path to the top was severe, steep and rocky, and many portions of the route were impossible to cycle. It was a case of climbing and clambering over rocks with the bikes on their shoulders.

There were walkers struggling to get to the top in various places along the way and Chris and Ian had to pass them with mountain bikes to carry. On the first day they spent half their time carrying their bikes over rocks.

With the descent as steep as the ascent, they both knew they would have to carry the bikes down again. By this time, Chris had become very frustrated with the ride. He felt he had spent more time walking and carrying the bike than riding. This was one of their last major rides together before their trip to the Himalayas. With so much walking Chris wasn't riding enough miles on the bike. As a result of his frustration Chris chose an alternative route down the hill. The route was far too steep; just as in North Wales Chris fell over the front of his handlebars and he tumbled with the bike down the hill. Even though the hill was grassy there were rocks and boulders, which made the fall scary. Luckily, apart from a few scratches and bruises, Chris emerged uninjured.

When they awoke the next day the rain was lashing down. They called off their plan to cycle over another mountain. Instead they decided to stay mostly on tarmaced roads rather than tracks, and cycle up the Kirkstone pass, a very steep road. It was hard going, but the terrain was superb for the first couple of hours. They followed a forested track alongside a fast-flowing brook, the water burbling over the rocks, before they had to join the road. Then the driving rain in their faces made the going even tougher. As they

Chapter 2 Energy

reached the top, and then moved into a downhill run, Chris sped off and became stuck behind a vehicle doing thirty miles per hour. The driver had spotted Chris and braked. Chris was going far too fast downhill in pouring rain on a bike of dubious roadworthiness. As he slammed on his brakes, his wheels locked and the back end of the bike skidded around at ninety degrees. Ian looked on aghast as Chris overtook the car, all the while wobbling behind his handlebars.

It was then that Ian realised he was cycling with a madman. He knew that he himself wouldn't have tried anything like that and for a brief moment he thought it would end in disaster, and there would be an outcome involving an ambulance. Chris later explained that he thought that the car had been accelerating at the time and it was only after the event when he looked at his own speedometer and saw that he had reached forty two miles per hour that he realised he could have really hurt himself.

It was becoming apparent that the two men had very different capabilities as cyclists. As soon as a significant incline appeared Ian would get into a very strong rhythm and slowly move away from Chris. Chris would plod along slowly and not keep up the pedal rate. It was clear that Chris was in no way an experienced cyclist.

They were both developing their stamina but each in completely different ways. Ian would go and go and go, where Chris would go, stop and recover, and then go, stop and recover. Even when they reached the Himalayas they noticed this more. Ian would always be in front on the long gradual climbs, whereas on the rides that undulated with short steep climbs Chris took the lead. Downhill, regardless of the terrain, and often more technical and rough, became Chris's forte, which he attributed to his experience as a downhill skier.

As the two prepared to head back home after their Helvellyn trip, Ian said, "I think we should both keep a log of the key things that we learn from the adventure, not just the blog we were going to write but something that would be useful for us to remember in life and in business."

Chris agreed this was a good idea. They both thought about how their physical condition was not yet right for their cycling challenge ahead. They took into account their differences and what they needed to do to prepare to get into a better condition.

They thought hard and wrote their first key observation: **'You can't do anything without your health'**.

Chapter 2 – Energy

Day 1 - Delhi to Pathankot

Ian and Chris touched down in New Delhi at half past two in the morning on a Friday; despite the early hour the airport was packed full of people rushing around, extremely busy. It seemed to the Europeans, who had never been to India before, that there was a fascinating contrast between the abundance of modern technology in evidence, and the apparent chaos of their surroundings.

They had arranged for their guide to meet them at the airport. "Can't see our man Ankur here yet" said Chris. "No," agreed Ian. "Let's wait for him in the arrival lounge."

After half an hour their curiosity got the better of them, and they stepped outside the building. A wave of heat hit them and nearly knocked them off their feet. The clamour of people was disorientating after the long flight. Back inside, they stood under the only fluorescent light, which did little to illuminate the space, and hoped that Ankur would be able to spot them.

A little while later he did. He was a fresh-faced young man, with a slightly nervous expression. It was clear he was anxious to please his first ever European customers.

They were expecting to travel north by train, as they had arranged back in the UK. However, Ankur told them at this point that they would be driving by road into the foothills of the Himalayas, a considerable distance from

Delhi and that it would take about fourteen hours. The prospect of a long drive after the plane journey was not what they wanted to hear.

They went outside to the support vehicle, a seven-seater spacewagon, and Ankur introduced them to Mukesh the driver. Next he proudly presented the two brand new bikes that he had bought the previous day. Ian and Chris looked at them with alarm. They were the sort of bottom-of-the-range bike you could buy at any hardware store in the UK, for not much money. Ian glanced at the heavy bikes taking note of the cast iron frame, aluminium rims, and the rear shock absorber, a steel spring the size of his hand which was adjusted by screwing a big nut to make it more or less absorbent. As they sat on the bikes the pedals were big and fat.

The size was perfect for Ian; as he was five feet six inches tall the bike fitted him and was comfortable. Chris however was well over six feet in height and found the bike far too small for his stature. It was by now five o'clock in the morning and impossible to make an exchange.

"Are we really going to ride these into the Himalayas?" Ian wondered aloud incredulously. Chris said "I don't think we've any option. I'll adjust the saddle and move the handlebars, to see if that makes any difference." After ten minutes, "no, there's still not enough leg room. I don't understand why we weren't fitted for the bikes at a rental store, but there you go, we'll have to cope with this."

Meanwhile, Ankur and Mukesh were delighted with the bikes, and didn't seem to notice Ian and Chris's reaction. So, they loaded the bikes onto the roof of the support vehicle and secured them under hessian sacking. With limited time they needed to get going, as they had a long drive ahead of them.

As they drove north from Delhi, an excited Chris exclaimed every ten minutes, "This is amazing!" and "wow, look at this". The drive was long and slow which gave them a chance to witness more of their beautiful surroundings and take in the hustle and bustle of the country. There were people everywhere like bees in a hive, small mopeds carrying as many as five passengers, cows wandering at will in the road and ponies pulling carts of produce piled impossibly high. They continued past fields where people looked for places to squat and relieve themselves, something they would never see in Western culture. They were filled by a strong sense of having landed in a different world.

During the journey, Chris and Ian discussed the purpose of their adventure with their new team. They made it clear that it was important to them to complete each stage of the journey on their bikes, and that they must reach the home of the Dalai Lama on day 8. Ankur confirmed the roles of the support team: he himself had taken care of the logistics, mapped out the route with the overnight stops, and would provide local knowledge, acting as interpreter. Makur the driver would manage their luggage, transport them safely, and set up camp for them.

A third member of the team would join them at their first overnight stop in the Himalayas. Ankur explained: "Because timing is so important to you, I don't want to take any chances with your stomachs and the local food, so it's best we have our own cook. We must always think about *safe* food". Ian and Chris were impressed; they'd never had their own cook before. It was clear that the safety of their

Chapter 2 Energy

guests was of paramount importance to the support team, and the two intrepid cyclists felt in good hands. However, the street food stalls lining the road at their stopping places were so tempting with their alluring aromas and colourful wares - it was all Chris could do to stop himself from buying and eating great quantities. Ankur was on hand to remind him of 'safe food' every time.

Stopping every few hours for safe food and refreshments they eventually reached Pathankot, a travel hub in northern India. As they arrived and stretched their tired legs from the car ride, they were eager to start their adventure.

They spent the evening touring the town, and exploring the fascinating markets, riding in a motorised rickshaw at great speed down the central shopping area. The skill of the driver was fantastic, dodging people and other rickshaws by the narrowest of margins. He nipped into non-existent gaps and swerved at the last minute to avoid a crash; it seemed like an action sequence from a James Bond movie.

Ramshackle shops selling exotic and spicy food, clothes and even bicycles lined the main street full of people, cars and rickshaws. Adjoining alleyways had much less traffic but they were still teeming and bustling with people. The air echoed with the noise of the traffic, the chatter of people and the smell of the produce on display.

The place where they were staying overnight was a fairly basic hotel with limited facilities. However, Ian and Chris slept like babies due to the long plane journey, the fourteen hours drive and their relief at arriving finally at the start point of their big adventure.

Day 2 - The start: Pathankot to Bharmour

Early next morning, after nearly three days of travelling, they now stood with their mountain bikes in the foothills staring into the beauty of the Himalayan range.

Sandy-coloured outcrops of rock tumbled away into the valley, against a backdrop of undulating hills, with tussocks of yellowy green grass waving gently in the slight breeze. Looking back the way they had travelled the day before, they could see wider open spaces, pastures, an altogether greener landscape. Ahead of them lay the taller mountains, green turning to grey, with jagged rock faces. The road they were standing on, their cycling start-point, wound around the side of the mountain, with a slope down to the river in the valley below. The sky was a brilliant blue, dotted with puffs of white cloud, and the sun was shining, glistening on the river water, that rushed over the rocks and provided the sound-track to the start of their adventure. This was it, the culmination of almost twelve months of planning and hard training; their excitement was palpable and they were raring to go.

Half an hour before, they had asked their guide Ankur various questions about the terrain, the distance and the height they would cycle on this first real day of their cycling adventure.

"What height are we going to gain over the day?" Ian asked Ankur. " About two hundred metres," Ankur replied.

"Are you sure, can you show me on a map please?" Ian asked. "I can't show you on a map," responded Ankur, "but it's two hundred metres."

"It's going to be a doddle today!" Ian said to Chris.

They set off with enthusiasm and excitement and a high level of energy. After three days of being cooped up in aeroplanes and then in the car, and sure in the knowledge that there was no big climb to worry about, they wanted to stretch their legs and release their energies. They were sprinting more than jogging, so to speak. At this stage the terrain looked almost disappointingly easy.

Ankur had instructed them to follow the main path. But from time to time, given they had no great challenge ahead, they explored interesting sidetracks which led nowhere, and then turned back to the main path. The blazing temperature was in the high twenties celsius, and they continued at a fairly brisk pace. They had been training hard, but the element they had been unable to practise back in the UK was the altitude. Ian thought that a forty kilometre ride with this level of ascent was a good first day, especially due to the fact they hadn't ridden now for three or four days. The ride turned out to be a gradual climb throughout the whole day, as the road undulated with short steep hills and drops, overall gaining about 200 metres in height.

Pushing through the heat of thirty degrees they cycled along taking in the breathtaking scenery. Surrounded by radiant mountains and coming across the occasional temple they rode alongside the River Ravi, punctuated by hydroelectric dams. Quaint little villages on the other side of the river were linked to the main road by bridges.

After about two hours of cycling, they came to a wooden suspension bridge over the river linking just such a small village to the road. "Good place to stop for a short break," said Ian. "Yes," agreed Chris. "I think we need to recharge our batteries."

The altitude, heat and continual climb were starting to take their toll. As they relaxed, they saw a wedding party come across the bridge. The happy young newly-married couple and the rest of their party assembled at the bus stop on the road. When the bus arrived, the bride and the women got into the bus taking their seats, while the groom and the men of the party clambered on top of the bus roof. The couple then set off for their first night of being married, and for the first night of the rest of their lives.

By late afternoon and getting tired, the two cyclists stopped in a small village, consisting of a line of shacks and brick houses either side of the road for two hundred yards, and had tea outside a small wooden hut. While the tea wasn't part of the Twining's range, it was probably the best tea Chris had ever tasted and was exactly what he needed. They knew at this point they had the final section of the day's journey left and they would have to start making their way to the hostel that had been arranged for their first evening. Ankur pointed them down into the valley to a bridge that crossed the ravine and then to a road up the other side that climbed severely as it clung to the edge of the sheer mountain. Ian jokingly said to Ankur, "I suppose that's where we're going next?" To which Ankur shook his head in agreement, in that Indian manner so confusing to foreigners that looks like "no" but usually means "yes". Chris and Ian stared at one another aghast. Another ten kilometres and an ascent of seven hundred and fifty metres stood between this cup of tea and dinner with a bed where they could rest for the night.

"Ankur, why didn't you tell us how hard this was going to be? You said two hundred metres of uphill cycling when we asked you this morning." Ian could barely keep the frustration and disappointment out of his voice. "I didn't tell you because I wanted to keep you motivated," was Ankur's response.

During the climb, the sun started to drop and darkness fell in behind them quickly. Tiredness was setting into their aching limbs. They kept going, determined to make the first night's destination on the bikes, but they had lost their level of trust and confidence in Ankur. They carried on going up and up until it became unsafe to continue, at which point the support vehicle came to rescue them. With heavy hearts and the bikes loaded on the roof they jumped into the back of the car. Their initial feeling was of tremendous disappointment that they hadn't reached their first checkpoint on two wheels.

"I'm gutted that we didn't make it," said Ian. "But what could we have done differently?" asked Chris. "We were given the wrong information, and we're dead tired due to the heat and the continual climbing. Had we known to start with about the steep climb at the end, we would never have taken all those little detours at the beginning. We always knew the Himalayas would be a challenge, and they certainly are."

Chris perked up, "We still have a lot to celebrate. We're in this fantastic place, which is where we planned to be."

They reached the hostel where they were to spend the night. It was on the outskirts of the village, a structure of rough brickwork scaling up to four floors, perched precariously on the side of the mountain. Both their rooms had "interesting" electrical wiring, which looked like the electricity supply might be a little erratic.

Ankur introduced another member of the support team, Dinesh the cook, who joined the party at this point. Dinesh went off into the hostel kitchen and rustled up a vegetable curry with fresh chapattis.

Ian and Chris sat in the hostel dining-room after the meal, drinking a bottle of very aptly named 10000 beer and pondered what they had experienced during the day.

"That was a really tough day," concluded Chris. "But there are things to learn from this. I think we can add another line to our book of learning,"

They added '**Achieving your goal requires physical, mental and emotional energy**' to the book.

And with that, they retired for the night, a thousand metres higher than they had anticipated.

Chapter 3 – Authenticity

Achieving your purpose in life requires the honesty to define your own authenticity - that is, know who you are and what you want

Day 3

The next day started well. It didn't bother either of them that they were at a greater altitude than they had anticipated, because as they awoke they stared down from a world heritage site into the outstanding views a thousand metres down the valley. It was simply stunning. As they had arrived late and after dark they had lost the sense of the landscape and the perspective in which they were travelling. At night, they had not been able to see that their rundown hostel was actually built into the side of a ravine. Now in full daylight, a perfect picture was framed through the hole in the wall that served as a window.

Chris thought to himself, "The countryside in England is beautiful and there are places where you can see rolling hills, and sometimes even mountains, but even in the remotest of areas you always get a sense that people are not far away." Chris was in awe of the view here; nothing man-made at all, there were no electric pylons running through the middle to blot out the beautiful landscape. Bright colours flooded in, the piercing blue of the sky and the lush green of the mountains. They were so high up above the ravine they could not see the bottom.

"You have to come and see this, Ian," Chris called. Ian stepped into the room, and could instantly see from a distance why he was here. He was silent. They both stared through the window, taking in the world as it was intended to be before starting their day.

Before they set off, the cyclists asked Ankur again about the terrain, the distance and the height they would climb on their bikes during their third day. Ankur was clear again in his response: it was to be downhill to where they had the tea stop the previous day, and then continuing down a steep road.

They had a walk around the village, and then at about half past nine in the morning they set off. The start of the ride went down the hill, back along the same route as they had cycled up the night before. Approximately a thousand metres' ascent the day before had taken the pair a good couple of hours although getting down took them only thirty-five minutes. They had a wry smile when they reached the bottom.

From the bottom of the valley they started to climb up the other side heading towards Holi. For two hours they cycled uphill only. It was marginally hotter on this particular day at just over thirty degrees Celsius, and at times this was pleasant and at other times stifling. They were both going well. This was in spite of the fact there were no fences along the roadside and five hundred metre drops. The roads were also used by bus drivers who drove unnervingly fast around the bends, which made Chris and Ian's ride for the day a little more challenging, and occasionally made their hair stand on end.

The ride distance was shorter than the day before at fifty kilometres and they arrived in Holi at half past three that afternoon. It was a tiny market village where the local men gathered around them when they stopped; the women looked on from afar. The villagers had many questions: their first question was how many gears did the bikes have? When they were told twenty-four gears, they were amazed. Everyone they met was so friendly, and wanted to know where they came from and why they were visiting.

There was nowhere to stay in the village and the support team had gone ahead to find a suitable place to camp by the side of a river. By the time Ian and Chris arrived, the cook had set up his kitchen on the river's edge.. Pots and pans were perched on rocks over an open fire, and a bright yellow tarpaulin served as a roof. Tea and biscuits were served on the rocks and the cyclists basked in the glorious afternoon sun.

A group of local boys spotted them arrive and came down to join them, happily smiling all the time. They clearly wanted to play on the bikes but Chris and Ian agreed it was best not to allow that in case they cycled over a cliff or into the river. Two of them were very chatty, Monu and Anil, speaking in Hindi. Given that the foreign cyclists spoke in English, neither party had a clue what the others were saying but it really didn't matter; good humour transcended the language barriers.

Chapter 3 Authenticity

Dinesh, the cook, prepared a tasty two-course dinner that evening using only the open fire. Feeling full and contented, Ian, Chris, Ankur and Dinesh sat around their own campfire and lay back looking at the stars in the clear sky.

Ankur asked "Would anyone like to sing?" Chris and Ian were taken aback. With no immediate response, Ankur continued: "OK, I'll start. This is a beautiful song about a boy who meets a girl and falls in love, then they are forced apart, and eventually they find eternal happiness." He proceeded to sing the Hindi song in good voice.

Inspired by that, Ian volunteered to sing next, ruining the peace and tranquillity. He gave his rendition of Elvis's 'Suspicious Minds', including a full demonstration of the legendary gyrations and hip-swivelling movements that had worked so well for Elvis. Chris rolled about the floor in hysterics, and Ankur was completely taken aback. Ian explained that he was going to enter the European Elvis singing championships in Blackpool when he got back to the UK. Ankur commented later that he loved the enthusiasm with which Ian sang, though they both chuckled.

Ian and Chris retreated to their tent at about ten o'clock that evening and fell asleep to the rhythmic sound of the river flowing beside them; they were so exhausted even the hard ground felt comfortable.

Day 4

Early in the morning, one of the local boys they'd met the day before put his head into the tent and loudly exclaimed "Good morning!" which woke them up with a start. Then Dinesh arrived with a welcome cup of tea.

As Ian poked his head out of the tent he couldn't believe his eyes: five hundred goats were herded right in front of them. "What a fantastic natural start to the day," he thought, "and how very different to my usual urban commuting life".

They had toast and tea for breakfast, sitting by the embers of the fire. The two local boys came and joined them and tucked into the breakfast too. With Ankur as interpreter, they told Ian and Chris about their homes on the mountain and their school, and they wanted to know all about England.

The day's ride began with fifteen kilometres of a particularly steep uphill climb of which the first three were really hard as their legs were stiff after two days of cycling. Added to that, they were saddle-sore and had to ride standing up. The sun was scorching down on them yet again. As they went higher the views became ever more glorious. It was simply the most refreshingly beautiful place in the world either Chris or Ian had ever seen.

They were making their way to Nayagran, the last settlement accessible by road at the head of the valley. Nayagran was in a stunning location at the confluence of three valleys. The road suddenly stopped, leading to the only visible building, the Lakewale Temple. On a rocky outcrop, a low white wall encircled a small stone building

Chapter 3 Authenticity

about ten feet square in the centre of the space. They could see a number of people inside the temple precinct, and hear them singing. It looked like a wedding was taking place at the temple. "Ankur, do you think it would be OK for us to visit the temple while the wedding is taking place? Or would that cause offence?" asked Ian. "No, indeed the wedding party would be pleased to welcome you travellers as honoured guests," replied Ankur. So, with a nod of agreement from Ankur, Ian and Chris entered the temple precinct.

They removed their mountain biking shoes and placed them with all the other footwear at the entrance to the temple as is an Indian tradition and then they joined the wedding ceremony that was taking place inside.

The temple building was open to the elements with a small sheltered area where the bridal party sat cross-legged on the floor. The women and young girls of the wedding party were sitting next to a small area at the centre of the temple with a golden statue of the goddess princess Lakewale. Dressed in brightly coloured saris, they filled the air with a melodious song, and an overwhelming sense of happiness.

The meeting with the Holy Man

The two visitors, and Ankur, were invited to take seats amongst the elders, who were sitting on a raised platform with a corrugated iron roof, in a corner of the surrounding wall. Chris sat down to the right of the groom's grandfather. The presiding Hindu priest, known as the

Pujari, peeled and sliced an apple and shared it among everyone who each took a small piece.

The Pujari then asked if anyone would like to ask a question. Ian had previously mentioned to Chris a year ago during their planning for the trip what he would ask when they finally reached the destination at the home of the Dalai Lama. Ian had wanted to ask his question as it seemed fitting that at the end of their journey they would be enlightened with some words of wisdom. Surrounded by the soft angelic voices of the women singing, Ian asked:

"As a matter of fact there is something I want to ask - why are we here and what is it all about?"

The Pujari smiled and started to recite from a sanskrit text, and then gave a response:

"Each and every one of us has been especially chosen to come to this place, this world, for a special purpose"

That wasn't quite enough for Ian as he wanted to know when he had achieved his purpose, so he followed up with a second question: "How do you know if you have achieved your special purpose?"

The Pujari responded, which was again translated for them by Ankur.

"You will know in your HEART. Your heart is full of goodness. It's what *you* think, not what someone else thinks, that is important. Your heart and mind are totally responsible if you are honest to yourself. Being honest is how you know you have got there."

In turn, the Pujari put the questions back to Ian, for him to consider for himself. Turning to Ian, Chris said, "This is so very special" and Ian nodded agreement, overwhelmed with emotion. Both men shed a small tear, and Chris continued: "You've been able to ask your burning question of a holy man in this wonderful place. I know this is why you came here." Ian had expected that he would be able to ask this question once they reached their destination. This was only day four, and already he had fulfilled one of his goals. Finding out the meaning of life was a pretty amazing thing for them both.

They left the temple and the wedding with full hearts. They set off back towards Holi where they had stayed the night before. In the town, bustling with local people visiting the colourful stores, they were cycling through when Ankur suddenly jumped out in front of them. Applying their brakes quickly Chris and Ian screeched to a halt and managed not to crash into him. Ankur told them they did not have far to go before the next stopping place, so they should take it easy. But they were so full of elation at finding out the meaning of life that adrenalin took over, and they continued at full speed down the hill. A few hours later the support vehicle caught up with them and Ankur jumped out to tell them that they had cycled past where they were going to be camping for the night.

Meanwhile, Chris was keen to send the latest dispatch for his blog back to base in the UK. For this, he needed a mobile phone signal. They loaded up the bikes and got in the car; about thirty minutes further on they found the signal and all was well with the latest blog posts. Chris didn't want to disappoint his many readers, or make his family anxious if they didn't get their daily reports.

Blog done, they drove back again and stopped next to a track leading through the woods. The track led down a very steep rocky bank, through grand trees, finally emerging onto the edge of the stunning river Ravi. The riverbed was made up of small stones and massive boulders where tranquil pools formed. Around the river there were shingle beaches and then steep slopes up to a grass flood plain.

It was a beautiful spot. Ankur, Dinesh and Makur had worked hard to set up the tents and cooking equipment on the shingle beach, just a few metres from the water. When Ian and Chris saw the location, they discussed with Ankur whether they should stay there, or if they should move a little further away. It was tempting to stay on the beach. But Ian said, "If there is any rainfall in the mountains the whole lot will get swamped". Ankur agreed that it wasn't worth taking the risk, even though there was no rain forecast. The hard work of moving everything began.

So they set up camp in a small clearing in the trees, next to the path about a hundred metres further up the hill. Dinesh prepared a delicious dinner once again, and they settled down for the night in this idyllic location.

Summary

That night Ian and Chris considered what they had learned over the previous two days; it had been fantastic and needed to be put in the book.

Achieving your purpose in life requires the honesty to define your own authenticity: that is, knowing who you are and what you want.

Chapter 3 Authenticity

Chapter 4 - Resilience

You need to take the knocks and handle the challenges on your journey

Day 5 Gorola to Himalayan Orchards

They had camped in a small wood on a steep slope. Waking up to unfamiliar sounds, Ian put his head out of the tent and saw two donkeys with bags full of rocks from the riverbed being led up the path between the tents. "Goats one day, donkeys the next, and tomorrow?" he thought to himself. The rhythm of the fast-running river in the background and the smell of breakfast cooking made him glad to be alive.

After a hearty breakfast they set off cycling towards the regional market town of Chamba, down the precipitous road which, although it was just a gentle downhill slope, was narrow and bordered by an alarming drop on one side. They were in no hurry and had time to appreciate the breathtaking scenery and enjoy the warm sun on their faces.

Things got a bit harder at Chamba with some steep climbs. At around four o'clock in the afternoon Ankur told Ian, "There's another five hundred metres to climb and a ten mile cycle up to the eco-friendly hotel of Himalayan Orchards." Chris was getting tired and his back was aching due to the ill-fitting bike. Finally, they reached the end of the track on their bikes. At this point Ankur told them there was a further ten minutes to walk up to the hotel. "You need to go straight up a very steep track, over a river, through some fields and then through a wood onwards and upwards."

Thirty minutes later, after a near vertical climb, they reached the top of some steps in a clearing, and could see the hotel. By this time, Chris could hardly move, his legs ached as never before and he was exhausted. The hotel looked very inviting, with lawns, a plunge pool, gardens dotted with ornamental trees and sunflowers, and stunning views across the valley.

The hotel staff greeted Ian and Chris with a warm welcome, and delicately placed orange spots on their foreheads. This tranquil place was just what they needed to recharge their batteries. An evening of good food, a dip in the pool and the prospect of a good night's sleep ahead, Chris and Ian retired early to gather their energy for the cycle to Jot the following day.

Day 6 - Himalayan Orchards to Jot

Their sixth day was going to be challenging as it involved cycling up to nearly four thousand metres; Ian and Chris knew it would be hard and that they would have to scale the highest mountain of their trip.

By half past eight in the morning the pair had set off on their journey to Jot. Beginning with ten miles of downhill cycling, Chris and Ian agreed that this was a dandy start to the day, although the next eight were uphill. When they reached the town of Chamba, Ankur proposed a tour of the

Chapter 4 Resilience

temples. They walked through some of the local market streets where cows ambled freely along the road and eventually they came to a temple complex.

The precinct housing a cluster of different sized plain stone buildings was largely empty of people. Each small building was a temple, with statues of deities inside. A holy man sat on the floor inside one temple, rapt in meditation. Away from the hustle and bustle of the town, Ian had a keen sense that this was a very special and holy place.

Climbing the highest mountain

Then Ankur took them to the road that would be the next part of their journey. As they both looked up at the route that lay ahead, they could see this was going to be especially difficult.

They stopped for a light lunch of dried fruit, nuts and water. Not long after they had started riding again, Chris found himself suffering an acute pain in his right knee every time he pushed down to pedal. He had no other option but to stop. Ian knew what to do: he made Chris bend his knee while he massaged it and the tendon surrounding the kneecap. This was serious. It was threatening to end Chris's journey on the bike altogether. Chris was thoroughly upset at the thought that he might not realise his goal.

However, he urged Ian to press on without him, "Ian, set your own pace for this next section, and I'll catch up eventually." Chris didn't know if he would make it to the check-point.

A few years previously, while in San Diego at a business conference, he had come across Reiki, a form of spiritual healing from Tibet, which he studied for a short time at the conference. He knew what to do, that the basic principle was about the power of the mind to overcome pain, as well as to alleviate it physically through warmth. He decided to give it a go, as he had nothing to lose. Surely in this place, so close to its origins, it was fitting to put Reiki into practice? So he cycled on, one hand on his painful knee to provide the warmth, and focussing positive thoughts to block out the pain from his consciousness.

The Reiki seemed to help, so Chris carried on cycling, keeping a slow and steady rhythm.

In six hours, Ian made it to the top, where he was met by a cheering crowd who were excited to see the strange sight of a European cyclist entering the village. Meanwhile, Chris was passing through each village where people stopped and stared at him, amazed by what they witnessed. Ankur spoke to the local people and discovered that no-one had ever seen a mountain bike come up that hill.

As the light started to fade, Chris was still ten miles away, and time was turning against him. He was determined to make it, nothing was going to stop him, and he pushed through the pain and tiredness. As local children ran through each village and followed him for a few kilometres this really helped to motivate him. Followed by a little girl and her younger brother panting and gasping for breath but both smiling all the time, Chris felt able to make the last push to finish his journey.

Chapter 4 Resilience

He carried on, having a few rest stops with bananas and juice. He passed a sign, just ten kilometres to go, then nine, and then eight. He knew he was reaching the final leg of his journey. Darkness was creeping in behind him, and he was acutely aware of the sheer drop over the cliff on the side of the road. The support car came down the mountain towards him; Ian hopped out and told him it was only two kilometres left. Chris was determined to continue, spurred on by cheers from the vehicle and Ian shouting encouragement all the way. He shed a tear, holding back from starting a flood so he could see where he was going. He knew the end of the journey was by now only a short ride away. The support car then followed behind, the lights on full beam leading Chris to the end of the day's cycle, where he collapsed in relief. Chris did not regard himself as a natural athlete so this was a massive achievement for him.

The ride to Jot was a huge challenge for Chris and he knew it would not have been possible without the team working with him. Over the course of eight hours' cycling relentlessly uphill where even the shallow inclines were a struggle, with the sun beating down on his back, Chris drank eleven litres of water. Ankur supplied him with more water and nibbles of food periodically, which allowed him to focus on his effort. The support team had made the impossible possible.

As he lay there on the floor, much like an exhausted marathon runner weeping with a barrel-full of emotions, Chris knew he had made it and conquered not only the most straining and draining journey of the trip but also of his life.

The pair had climbed one thousand eight hundred and fifty metres. They had both pushed through the pain barrier and finished, and now it was time to enjoy some food, and a "10000" beer, which sounded just a little too appropriate. On the journey Chris had been fantasising about eating some noodles for dinner, and he was in luck: it was noodles.

Day 7

Back on the bikes again the next morning, things started badly when Ian became frustrated with his brakes, which had started to bind; the brakepads were pressing against the wheel which had the effect of applying the brakes unintentionally. He found himself working a lot harder than he should have been and he tried to adjust the brakes in preparation for the forthcoming downhill stretch. Unfortunately the end of the spindle snapped, which secured the back wheel to the frame of the bike.

What could they do? It was time for Ankur to come to the rescue. He found a local man who figured out a way to repair the spindle using a nut from a big plastic sweetie jar full of assorted nuts, bolts and washers, and the bike was just about roadworthy once again, allowing them to continue down the hill. In fact the back wheel was held in place by just one quarter turn of the spindle thread. Ian made his mind up this time to ignore the binding of the wheel on the brake.

Their cycling on this journey overall was built around climbs and descents; Ian was faster on the climbs and Chris faster on the descents. Given their setbacks today, they were running a little behind schedule. Ian made the

Chapter 4 Resilience

mistake of suggesting that they should have worked on a faster pedal rate on his ascents, just before the gears started slipping. Chris sped off downhill, leaving Ian behind.

Three-quarters of an hour later Ian had caught up with Chris, and the two now enjoyed some well-deserved lunch and a short break.

Preparing to set off for the afternoon, Ian noticed the back spindle had come undone again and it was not possible to repair it on the spot. Limping into the next village, the pair found a mechanic who kindly welded the bike back together for Ian.

Now it was time to head back onto the main highway. Just before they set off, they discussed how the setbacks they had faced today could have impacted on their goal to reach Dharamshala. Determined to get there, Ian and Chris headed straight for Dharamshala and before they knew it the day's journey was over. Ian and Chris had made it where they wanted to be.

Summary

They thought about the challenges they had needed to overcome over the course of their adventure.

- Working with bad equipment - It started with the cycles
- Physically enduring climbs - particularly tough on the first and fourth days with the challenging climbs up to Bharmour and Jot

- The walk up to the hotel at Himalayan Orchards – Chris could hardly walk up the hill he was so exhausted
- The food – they had spent nearly a week eating nourishing but unfamiliar food - what they would have given for a steak and chips
- The culture – difficult to decipher instructions, and a lack of precision on what would be expected

It was time to write in the notebook again. Ian wrote:

You need to take the knocks and handle the challenges on your journey

Chapter 5 - Team

You can't do something special by yourself, you need to work with others and learn from others

The journey into Dharamshala was exciting. Not only had they reached their final destination of the trip, but there was a sense of arriving somewhere special. The military presence in the area, reflecting the proximity to the Chinese frontier, only added to the dramatic tension. Army barracks bordered the road, behind white brick walls and barbed wire, guarded by soldiers on the gates. The town itself was on a steep slope, and as you enter, you weave through steep hilly tracks lined with apartment buildings and shops.

Ian and Chris found their hotel, a rather run-down but spacious, old-fashioned establishment. To celebrate arriving at their destination, and the conclusion of their trip, they decided to drink wine with their evening meal. They found a bottle of red wine on sale in a local shop and bought it for a small fortune; the shopkeeper was having a good day. Back at the hotel, they took the bottle into the restaurant. When the waiter saw what they were carrying he ushered them to a table at the back of the dining room, wrapped the bottle in newspaper and asked the two of them not to be conspicuous. They happily complied, not wishing the hotel staff to get into trouble but at the same time determined to celebrate.

Day 8

The next morning they went out into the street, hearing the sounds of chanting coming from the many temples. The streets were busy with orange and maroon-clad monks and Tibetans, and a few young foreign backpackers strolled around. The main thoroughfare was low rise, with as many shops selling religious artefacts as groceries. Altogether, there was a relaxed and peaceful atmosphere.

Ian and Chris noticed large wooden devices outside each temple, painted cylinders that turned on a spindle, with sacred text carved into the wood; people would turn them to create musical prayers. They learned that these were Tibetan Buddhist prayer wheels.

All roads seemed to lead to the main temple, the home of the Dalai Lama, and they made their way there. The precinct was a beautiful open courtyard, where monkeys were swinging from the trees and ran across the corrugated roofs. Chris felt overwhelmed with tranquillity and peace; looking across to Ian he knew that deep down he felt this too.

The smell of incense filled the small central temple building, which was simple and unostentatious, with a beautiful highly polished wooden floor, just like a school hall at the start of term. One elderly monk sat with his back against the wall, chanting mantras. A woman arrived and set down her prayer mat. She knelt down, and then lowered her head to the floor, outstretching her arms. She returned to the kneeling position, and then repeated the movement over and over again. It felt like a very holy place combining spirituality with history. Statues surrounded the central space, where the Dalai Lama's

43   *Chapter 5 Team*

throne was positioned and covered with a simple cloth, only uncovered when His Holiness was present in the temple.

Many Tibetan people and monks were entering the temple. Chris sat down next to one of the monks, closed his eyes and found himself feeling at total and utter peace with the world.

This trip was inspired by the untimely death of Andrew Lee, Ian's good friend. Ian had carried Andy's order of funeral service on every practice bike ride, and now on this trip; this was the place he was going to leave it. He placed it on the throne of the Dalai Lama as a gesture of remembrance.

Returning to sit next to a Tibetan woman chanting her devotion to the Dalai Lama, Ian became overwhelmed with emotion, and time seemed to stand still for him. He could have spent hours listening to the mesmeric sounds around him. He reflected on his friendship, and how he hoped that Andy might have achieved reincarnation that would take him on a quest for enlightenment, as Buddhists believe. Tears flowed down his face. Chris encouraged him to let it out, and he did. He cried and cried for the injustice of his friend's early death.

Ian wanted to light a candle in memory of his friend. Chris too wanted to light a candle, though he wasn't sure why exactly. Ankur checked the protocol with the monks, and the two were ushered into a small room at the side of the temple. There they discovered it was customary to light not one but a hundred candles; it occurred to Chris that the repetition of the candle-lighting, the regularity of the activity over and over again, was similar to the chanting of a mantra and could lead to a trance-like state. It certainly reflected the impact of this holy place on their feelings, and was a fitting tribute to Andy.

How grateful they were. As they left, they reflected on their experience of this temple and their time in India. They had each achieved something special on this adventure, and to Ian it had become something of a pilgrimage: now they felt they had to share it.

Reflecting on their experience

Both found the experience together enriching. They don't describe themselves as explorers or adrenalin junkies, just as two straightforward chaps who work hard to achieve their goals, in life and in business.

The Himalayan adventure started out with three parts to the goal: to undertake something in memory of Andy Lee, to do something that was both challenging and fun, in keeping with Andy's approach to life, and to do something that combined both of the above with a spiritual element. Having completed their journey, Ian and Chris reflected that the experience did awaken a spiritual sense, as they visited such holy places and encountered deeply spiritual people. When Ian placed Andy's order of funeral service on the Dalai Lama's throne, he felt deeply moved; he could now let go of his grief.

They were near the end of the adventure, and had mixed emotions: feeling sad that the brilliant journey was over, yet feeling glad they had accomplished what they set out to do, and looking forward to sharing their stories with friends and family back home, who had given them so much support.

New Delhi via Taj Mahal

It was time to contemplate the journey back to New Delhi, to go to the airport. Neither was looking forward to that long car journey again, but they decided to break it up with a diversion to take in the Taj Mahal en route. The diversion turned out to be longer than expected, and to add another five hours in the car. However, given the Taj Mahal is one of the seven modern wonders of the world, and they were roughly 'in the vicinity', then they expected it would be worthwhile.

It was incredibly impressive and certainly worth the extra miles; both were glad they had seen it. But somehow, the comparison with the simple natural beauty of the past week in the mountains left Chris and Ian feeling just a tinge of disappointment, though they felt loth to admit it. The place was thronging with people, which came as a sharp contrast to the largely empty mountainsides, with small villages and friendly people, curious to see the two cyclists on their journey.

The following eight hours in the car back to New Delhi gave them plenty of time for further reflection on their achievement. They remembered the highs and lows of the adventure: waking up on the first morning to take in the wonderful mountain views; the exhaustion in reaching some of the checkpoints; the happy smiling face of the local boy peering into their tent to wake them up; the herds of goats and donkeys passing by; the conversation with the

46

holy man; the wedding parties; the problems with the
bikes, and the local people who marvelled at the 24 gears.

They had achieved their goals. For Ian, the trip had become
a pilgrimage in memory of his friend Andy Lee, and out of
his own grief he had created something marvellous. For
Chris, he had exceeded his fitness expectations to reach a
magical place in the Himalayas by cycling. Both felt they
had proved that if you really set your mind to achieving
something wonderful, then anything is possible.

For their last night in India, the support team took them to
a restaurant off the beaten tourist track, where they all
enjoyed a sumptuous Indian banquet, laughing and joking
together. It was a special treat as a thank-you from the
support team, who told Ian and Chris that they had helped
them achieve their own goal, of a successful trip with their
first European customers.

Summary

They took out the notebook and summarised another key
learning from the adventure:

**You can't do something special by yourself, you need to
work with others and learn from others**

Epilogue

Taking their seats on the plane very early the next
morning, they were both half asleep. Ian murmured that
Chris would now be able to write the book he had been
contemplating for some time, as the trip had given him so

Chapter 5 Team

much material. Chris grunted a response in the negative. Ian persisted, and Chris, just wanting to block out the sound and go to sleep, said: "If you want a book so much why don't you write it yourself?" At that moment they looked at one another and were wide awake: they should write the book together.

As soon as he could, Chris got his pad out of his backpack and started making notes, capturing their thoughts. Early into the flight, they already had 17 stories and anecdotes that were shaping up as metaphors for achieving success. A short while later, the HEART framework was born. And so, one adventure ended, and another one started, as this book developed and Ian and Chris found themselves in demand to speak at conferences.

Section 2

In your HEART in practice

Chapter 6 – Health

Be fit for success

You can't do anything without your health

Introduction

In business we train our minds with degrees and diplomas, attend time management courses and learn how to implement the most sophisticated project management systems in the hope of achieving better performance. That's all fine but the marathon of business life creates a bi-product: stress. To deal with stress requires a level of wellness covering diet, exercise, relaxation and stimulation, and sleep.

It would be considered absurd to go cycling in the Himalayas without the appropriate health or fitness, yet everyday millions of business people are working without the appropriate levels of health and are seriously impacting their performance as a result. Many writers refer to business as a marathon, yet who would run a marathon without training?

'Be fit for success' was a key element of the preparation for the Himalayas. Health and fitness was evident amongst the business leaders interviewed for this book, and they are essential to any person on the journey to success.

Health for the Indian adventure

From Chapter 1 we heard that Chris was a big chap whose walking consisted of the journey from his car to the front door of his house and he had never really cycled, and certainly he had never cycled up a mountain. He found his first cycle trip in Wales was something of a challenge as his body wasn't prepared for the ordeal.

On the other hand Ian had mountain-biked but knew he was not in the best shape at that time as he could have been.

They each set out on various trips, solo and together, testing their stamina for the challenge they faced in the Himalayas. They knew that without their health and fitness they couldn't do anything.

The preparation for the trip involved plenty of aerobic exercise for Ian, including running, tennis and cycling the Coast to Coast trans-Pennine cycleway in northern England, whilst Chris was beginning to develop his cycling stamina through weekly trips to the Bracknell forest in the south.

To ensure both men were fit enough they undertook a cycle ride over Helvellyn, the second highest mountain in England.

While they were in India the importance of health in achieving a successful outcome came to light:

- Ankur the guide had been asked take care of their diet. As a result of his care and advice, Ian and Chris ate only vegetarian food during their visit and did not suffer any stomach upsets. Both men ate for the journey they were taking, having a hearty breakfast, lunch and dinner with an afternoon snack. Despite this, they returned from the trip the lightest in weight they had been in years

- They ensured they had enough sleep and gave their bodies time to recover before the challenges of each day
- Although they had the occasional beer, the men were looking after their bodies by not drinking excessively
- The physical training enabled them to cycle the highest mountains and achieve the challenges

Wellbeing at work

Investing time in leisure and fitness activities or participating in relaxation techniques boosts your wellbeing. It is important for you personally, and the people you work with, your senior colleagues, the people who work for you, and your peers.

Research carried out by the British Heart Foundation showed that companies can protect their employees from the causes of long term sickness (coronary heart disease, stroke, obesity, type two diabetes, high blood pressure, stress, anxiety, osteoarthritis, osteoporosis and lower back pain) by promoting and encouraging exercise among their staff. Whether or not our employers are supporting us, we need to take responsibility for ourselves too.

Some estimates show that exercise can reduce your sickness absence by nearly 25%.

With the sheer volume of work and deadlines, 89% of managers admitted to working over and above their contracted hours on a regular basis. Taking sick leave is not an option for many. Compared to the average sickness absence of 6.7 days, CIPD reports revealed managers took a total of 3.4 days a year. With high workloads and pressure, they are running the risk of burnout, and are most likely not performing at their best.

13% of managers admitted to suffering from depression, and one in three claimed they felt stressed during work. Dr Jenny Leeser, Clinical Director of Occupational Health for Bupa, commented: *"This statistic may not be that much different from non-managers but it does give us a measure of the impact mental ill-health could have on the workplace."* She continues, *"Workplace pressure can affect everyone differently. For some employees it can be motivational; for others it can lead to physical symptoms such as headaches or muscular tension if not addressed early on, and these might cause absence. For some people the adverse effects of pressure can lead to depression and there is then potential for long-term absence."*

Looking after your health - practical guidance

It is important to note that we are not advocating that all readers should try to attain Olympic superstar status. We each have different physical abilities, and what is important is to work with what you have to maximise your health and fitness. Management literature and the wisdom of the business leaders we have interviewed suggest that you can make a real impact on your business performance if you look after your health. Individuals should develop their own health improvement plan: take time to examine your health and identify the few things you might do to make a real and lasting difference. A healthy body is a key building block to personal and business success.

Below are just three of the areas you might consider, and remember that these are highly interconnected: if you eat well and healthily, and exercise regularly, you are reducing your stress levels.

- **Plan your diet** – Analyse your diet, particularly your calorific content, types of food, vitamins, proteins, carbohydrates, fats and minerals. Also, look at what you drink – what is your caffeine intake (a very potent drug) and what is your alcohol and drug intake? From this insight identify who you want to be based on the food and drink you consume and put together an action plan to achieve this
- **Have an exercise plan** – How often and to what intensity are you exercising? What could you do to make a difference? It doesn't have to involve running a marathon. The difference might come from walking up stairs rather than taking the lift, though for others it might come from setting an exercise challenge such as running a marathon
- **Relax** – Your business performance will improve if you spend sufficient time on the things you enjoy and those activities that take the mind away from the stress of business and everyday life. Spend time analysing how you are living your life and identify the things that you enjoy. If your action plan involves diet and exercise so much the better. Relaxation techniques such as yoga or meditation may be the right approach for you, and time with the family is the perfect way to relax for others

The continual barrage of meetings, requests, calls and challenges in business life can, for many, invoke a physical response that makes them feel upset or threatened or out of balance. Stress can affect the mind, body and behaviour in many ways, and everyone experiences stress differently.

A stress response is perfectly natural and is designed to protect you. It keeps you alert when you need to stay focussed, and in an emergency it can save your life, so you react quickly to danger. In reasonable measures it is good for you: helping you perform in front of an audience, or boosting you to complete a piece of work for an important deadline.

Jane Madders, psychologist, says: "*It is when these normal and useful reactions are prolonged to become excessive and inappropriate that the trouble begins.*"

She tells how prolonged stress can have damaging physical effects: high blood pressure and cardiovascular disease, digestive disorders such as stomach ulcers and colitis, and a greater susceptibility to infections.

However, a certain level of stress is positive, and some theorists refer to this as 'arousal'. A degree of arousal creates the right environment for good performance and achievement. Too much arousal, or stress, leads to exhaustion and illness. Dr Peter Nixon, an eminent cardiologist, devised a human function curve where he mapped performance against arousal.

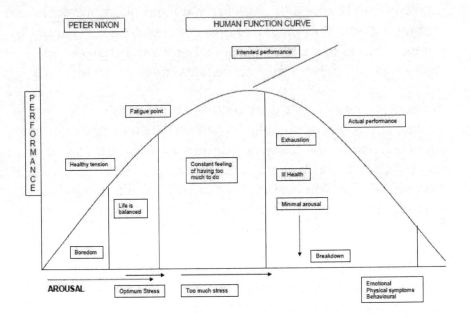

Another approach to health is put forward by Jagdish Parikh in his book '*Managing Your Self*'.

He describes five major ways in which you can manage your body, and enhance its potential: diet; exercise; breathing; recreation and relaxation; and achieving wellness.

Diet - Balanced nutrition is just as important as calorific intake

Exercise - There are so many types of exercise to choose from, that you must be able to find one that suits you

Breathing - You should pay more attention to technique: unless you entirely empty your lungs of impure air, you cannot draw in the maximum amount of *pure* air, which has consequences for the purification of the blood, and your overall wellbeing including your mental health.

Recreation and relaxation - These are great stress-relievers, and contribute to the health of various organs and systems in the body, including brain function. Sometimes a competitive attitude is not helpful, and people playing sport should remember to enjoy themselves rather than play to win every time

Achieving wellness - Actively manage yourself, to create a *"relaxed, radiant and energised body"*

Health is an important factor behind success for both the individual and the organisation. An enlightened business manager will not just focus on business goals but the health of his or her team. Here are three areas for a team manager to consider:

Be aware – Be tuned in and listen to others about their health improvement goals and look for opportunities to know more

Show interest – If an employee discloses a health-related goal, find out what matters most to support their success. Don't just listen, be an active listener

Give support - Share your own 'testimony of health', as a personal story can be one of the most powerful tools to emphasise your support. If you don't have a personal testimony of health improvement, endorse the wellness programmes offered by the company

10 Ways to Get More Exercise

BUPA, a leading private health care provider in the UK, publishes these useful tips on its website:

1. *Try out a few different activities until you find one you want to stick with – think about rock climbing, cycling, swimming or a team sport like netball or football*
2. *Exercise with friends or work colleagues for added motivation*
3. *Think of exercise as a great excuse for 'me time', away from all your daily pressures*
4. *Set yourself a goal – such as losing weight or preparing for a race – and picture yourself fitting into that special outfit or crossing the finishing line*
5. *Promise yourself tangible rewards that will encourage you to achieve these goals*
6. *If you're not a gym fan, try exercising somewhere different, like a forest, beach or park*
7. *Avoid short trips in the car, walk instead and, when taking the bus to work, get off a couple of stops early and walk from there*
8. *Use the stairs rather than the lift or escalators; you'll feel better for it*
9. *Put extra energy into your household chores (they'll be out of the way quicker too)*
10. *Keep it up – exercise improves health and fitness, gives you more energy and can help to reduce stress!*

Dr Tyler Cooper, writing in Texas CEO weblog, asserts:
"Fitness helps everyone live longer – moderate levels of exercise decrease the risk of dying from cancer by 58%, and exercise lengthens our lifespan by six to nine years."

Health in action

Peter Pastides makes a point about the importance of sleep for him:

"The worst thing in the world is chronic fatigue - you cannot continue to operate effectively and at the pace I operate at if you are fatigued. I need a good eight hours sleep, whether that's going to bed early, or later but waking up late the next day. I don't take sleeping pills, but I do make sure that I get a good rest so I can think quickly, move quickly, and meet the demands I put on myself and the teams I work with. Everybody needs rest."

He continues:

"I believe every second in the day is a gift. The way I live my life is that you can't have energy if you aren't fit, so I keep myself healthy. Balance is important: sleeping well, eating well, and exercising."

Sir Paul Judge believes in dietary moderation:

"I am lucky to be healthy and I try to stay healthy. I have always been food-conscious, and I eat and drink fairly normally. I gave up smoking 27 years ago."

Sometimes extra effort is needed. **Peter Pastides** again:

"At one point I needed to manage my weight, and lost tens of pounds. I started entering 10k's running, swimming, and mountain biking, and my energy and productivity transformed overnight. That's how I get my energy."

Paul Hewerdine makes the connection between physical and mental fitness:

"I like staying active so I play football. I've played with some guys who are still going well into their 50's and that gives me hope that I will still be playing for some time, even if I'm a little bit slower. I think that physical fitness is important for you mentally as well."

Philip Oliver has worked for many years in a corporate environment where he has seen people pushing themselves to the maximum. He knows this is sometimes necessary, but not sustainable over the long-term. He is clear on his beliefs with regard to health:

"Do not burn the candle at both ends for too long - and enjoy everything but not in excess"

Health in action: Chris

Chris has started his own company and has never worked so hard. It was particularly noticeable in the early days when the company was establishing itself, that Chris would attend meetings, networking events, run training sessions and consult with his clients, as well as the much loved business breakfasts, lunches and dinners. He was working too hard and for too long. Even though he recognised this was not good or sustainable, he was driven to pay the mortgage, and he'd learned that running your own business does not come with an off switch.

One of Chris's motivations for mountain biking across the Himalayas was the need to get fit and healthy. He is very goal-orientated and he knew that if he had a goal of cycling the Himalayas, he would build a health regime into his diary. The goal would force him to get some work/life balance.

Since his return, he has maintained his fitness and taken up tennis and swimming, as well as continuing to mountain bike. He is now far more conscious of what he eats. Chris doesn't always get it right and business lunches are still a part of the business schedule, though he keeps an eye on what he orders and makes sure he swims some extra lengths in the pool the next time to compensate.

Chris recognises his work performance improves when he eats well and exercises. He is constantly on his feet delivering training events for top-performing sales forces all over the world, and is a regular keynote speaker at conferences. Taking rest and making sure he has time to relax and enjoy himself is very important, so he always has the next holiday planned. He books time out to ensure that rest is built into his life. His clients expect world class training and consultancy, and Chris takes care to ensure he is at the top of his game for them.

Health in action: Ian

A few years ago Ian was diagnosed with 'raised intolerance to glucose', a condition that can lead to diabetes unless action is taken. Ian reasoned that his lifestyle, with many business lunches, too much alcohol, while overweight and with a tendency to work long hours, was having an impact on his body. He addressed his challenge by:

- Losing 14 pounds in weight through a healthier diet
- Taking lunch breaks whenever possible (and going road running)
- Increasing his exercise overall, with tennis, cycling, windsurfing and sailing

The outcome was that he lowered the amount of cholesterol and blood sugar in his body, and became fitter and healthier. He has kept his weight down and his last two medicals have shown that his blood sugar has returned to normal levels. What's more, Ian feels healthier and more ready to deal with the challenges of everyday business life.

References

'Well@Work' Loughborough University, 2009, used by the British Heart Foundation for 'Health@Work' programme

'Stress and Relaxation – self-help techniques for everyone' Jane Madders, MacDonald and company, 1979

'Human Function Curve' Dr Peter Nixon, 1979

'Managing Your Self – management by detached involvement' Jagdish Parikh, Blackwell, 1991

How Executives can shape their health and their company's future Tyler C Cooper MD, Texas CEO weblog, 2011

Chapter 7 – Energy

Channel your passion

Achieving your goal requires physical, mental and emotional energy

Introduction

Energy is the capacity of a physical system to perform work. Cars don't move without a well working engine and petrol or diesel. A high performance car needs much more than fuel: it needs the engine, tyres, suspension, steering, exhaust , electrics and so on to be tuned for success.

The human body is similar. We have already heard that health is an essential ingredient of success but the trick to optimising one's ability to perform work and succeed is based on focusing on and fine-tuning the four areas of energy you require to be successful: mental, physical, spiritual and emotional energy.

Knowing where your personal energy comes from and what triggers it is a true key to success. Typically this boils down to an awareness of and an ability to channel one's passion. It was something that the business leaders interviewed were very aware of and chimes with the research reviewed in this chapter.

Energy in India

In Chapter 2 we heard how Ian and Chris arrived in Delhi and found that the bikes were too small. You might argue that what was required was resilience but just as important was the mental energy to think clearly and to work out how to deal with the situation.

There are many examples of the requirement for physical energy in that story, from the afternoon cycle climb up to 2600 metres on the second day of the adventure to the physically gruelling ride up to Jot later in the week. The walk up to the hotel at Himalayan Orchards was particularly exhausting, calling on the final reserves of physical energy from both men.

There were other energy dynamics at work too: the conversation with the holy man at Lakewale temple fuelled an energy that can best be described as spiritual. In fact, it has inspired the writing of this book. The authors also felt surges of energy as they visited some of the holy places such as the temples in Dharamshala and Bharmour.

What can you do to manage your energy?

Tom Cox, business guru, created a list of *"Five steps to energy management"*, summarised here:

1. List the things that give you energy, and keep it visible on your desk. You might be tempted to stop doing these things when you feel overwhelmed - don't be
2. Work in sprints rather than one long set of marathon hours. If you have a day of back-to-back

meetings, you could be destroying your productivity

3. Intersperse your sprints with one or two things from your list of energy-giving activities. You'll build up your reserves if you take time out to recover

4. Take the pattern of sprint, relax, sprint, relax and build it into your ritual of behaviour so that it comes naturally to you

5. Do not multi-task during your sprint but focus on one demanding task at a time

Cultivate self-awareness and understand what drives you, which is part of your own *Emotional Intelligence (EI)*. There's a lot more on EI in Chapter 8, but meanwhile, consider the useful model for self-knowledge called the Johari Window.

Self-knowledge: the Johari Window

This model was developed by Joseph Luft and Harry Ingham in 1955.

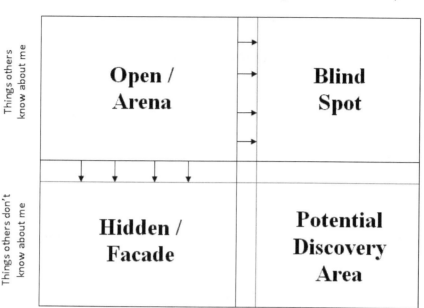

Bear in mind that it is desirable to increase the size of the arena, by pushing into the blind spot and façade windows.

Open/Arena

The arena is characterised by an open exchange with others of information about yourself that you are aware of. It increases in size as the level of trust grows between you and another person. The arena continues to get larger as a personal working relationship grows.

Blind Spot

The blind spot contains information that others know about you, but you don't know about yourself. We all communicate things to others that we are unaware of. We do this through mannerisms or our tone of voice. We all know someone who thinks they are the 'soul' of the party, when everyone else just thinks they are being a pain. Individuals characterised by large blind spots are known as: 'the bull in the china shop'.

Hidden/Façade

A façade consists of the things you know about yourself but do not share with others. These can be fears that if you openly discuss your feelings, opinions and perceptions, people will reject them or use them to attack you. This window is larger in teams where there is little support for one another. Individuals believe they will judged negatively after revealing their thoughts and reactions.

We cannot grow our arena without sharing information with others. We have to take a risk and share information so we can find out the reactions of those around us. People with a large façade window are often known as 'the clown', hiding behind a mask which is difficult to penetrate.

Potential Discovery Area

The fourth window contains information that no one knows, not even yourself. Traumatic experiences can reveal the hidden depths of someone's personality. On the other hand we have talents and potential that can be

Chapter 7 Energy

discovered by trying new experiences. These are things which we will find out about ourselves over time, reducing the Unknown window.

Building relationships with others

By reducing the size of our blind spot through seeking feedback from others we build effective working relationships. We also do this by revealing our true feelings, perceptions and opinions to others by providing considered feedback.

If you manage people

Maintain energy levels at meetings. Recognise that everyone needs energy and people operate at different levels. Structure meetings to have breaks and ensure that every meeting is a series of sprints, and not a marathon.

Suggest that people stop checking emails during meetings.

Fuel positive emotions in yourself and others. Teams that celebrate and share their emotions succeed where others fail. The leadership challenge is to channel these emotions and levels of success by regularly expressing appreciation.

Make sure the team understands its significance. Make sure each team member understands the significance of the team and the contribution of the individuals involved.

Managing your own energy

Writing in their book 'Energy is real', Gail Christel Behrend and Claudette Anna Bouchard describe four forms of energy: physical, emotional, mental and spiritual. Their research has led them to conclude that these forms interact and that with an understanding of these energy forms, people can achieve much more in life through health and happiness. Schwartz and McCarthy recommend a set of strategies to help executives better manage their energies. The definitions and management strategies are summarised below:

Physical energy

This is the energy sometimes referred to as 'life force' or 'vitality' and it provides us with energy sensations that deliver important images of how we are living our lives: for example, the endorphin rush at the end of a run or the wide-awake ready-to-go feeling after a good night's sleep and a healthy breakfast. At the other end of the scale tiredness, cold sweat, and rapid breathing all tell us something is amiss.

To manage it: getting a good night's sleep on a regular basis improves your energy. Go to bed earlier, and if you reduce your alcohol consumption it will have a positive impact on both sleep and energy. Think about your diet: rather than have infrequent heavy meals, eat light meals and healthy snacks every few hours. Engaging in cardiovascular activity at least three times a week and strength training once a week will have a beneficial effect. Just as important is to take regular breaks throughout the working day and appreciate when your energy levels are becoming low

Emotional energy

This form of energy is derived or used by the vast array of emotions that we experience: ranging from grief or jealousy on the negative side to positive emotions such as gratitude, love and joy.

To manage it, learn how to diffuse negative emotions such as irritability, impatience, anxiety and insecurity. Deep abdominal breathing is the way to do this; you are less likely to be stressed if you are breathing deeply.

Fuel positive emotions in yourself and people around you by regularly expressing appreciation to them in detailed and specific terms, through notes, emails, calls or conversations.

Mental energy

Our mental energy includes not only our thoughts but also our ability to think clearly, to reason, to analyse, to focus and to plan. It includes our intuitive mind, our memories, knowledge, techniques and skills we have learned as well as our ability to communicate clearly with others.

Your mental energy dramatically falls if you try to do too many things at once. You can significantly increase your mental energy by reducing interruptions and by performing high concentration tasks away from phones and email. Other tactics to consider include responding to voicemails and emails at designated times during the day.

Spiritual energy

This is the energy that gives us our sense of meaning and purpose; some call it the 'stirrings of the soul'. It can be an energy that causes man to move mountains, and includes our dreams, creative impulses, a sense of destiny or fate, inspiration, joy, love, values, ethics, conscience, a sense of purpose and our inner wisdom.

Identify your sweet spot activities: those that give you feelings of effectiveness, effortless absorption and fulfilment. Find ways to do more of these and delegate the things you don't enjoy to those who do enjoy them. Allocate time and energy to what you consider most important.

Our physical, emotional, mental and spiritual energies are not isolated, but they are linked to one another. They exist as part of a greater whole: Behrend and Bouchard call this our energy self. For example, often when people are low physically, perhaps because of a cold or illness, at the same time their emotional, mental and spiritual energies drop as well. That's why when we are sick we are likely to have pessimistic thoughts.

Energy in action: the business leaders' views

Many of the business leaders are energised by those around them. **Thomas Martin** says:

"I just work with some fabulous people. I was adding up, I've probably done between 1400 and 1600 visits to the Arco business units over the last 24 years and I can say every single time I've

*gone out to a branch or a part of the business I've learned
something. Every single time. The energy comes from that
discovery, from working with great people, from trying to do
different things, and do them better. It used to come from a desire
to prove myself but I've got over that now and people take me or
leave me for what I am."*

Chris Stock is a self-confessed extrovert, meaning that he
derives energy from the people he interacts with, in the
classic Myers-Briggs model:

*"I get my energy from being around people. If I look the Myers-
Briggs definition of introvert and extrovert I am a very strong
extrovert insofar as I get my energy from people, and I know that
to be true for me. I can be incredibly tired and then arrive at a
venue to do some training or a keynote speech and then, just
being around people in a vibrant atmosphere brings me alive. As
I step onto the stage I have all the energy and motivation I need."*

He's conscious that's not the same for everyone:

*"I need people around me as I get my energy from working and
leading a team. But I also take note of where the others in the
team get their energy. I work with a very talented executive
coach. When we work together on a training course, at the breaks
and lunchtime, she takes herself off to be alone for a while. Being
an introvert she needs to regain her energy that way."*

Recognising great teamwork, and the success of
individuals gives **Fergal Morris** an energy boost:

*" The thing that really stimulates my energy is seeing success or
seeing something I have worked on, and the team has worked on,
where we've put together a plan, we've executed the plan and it's
delivered what we wanted or more than what we wanted. I also*

get my energy from seeing people around me being successful. Nothing pleases me more than to see people taking on new responsibilities being successful and moving on or getting the rewards thus making a difference to them."

Leadership itself can be energising. **Fergal** continues:

"I'm quite competitive and I like to be at the front. I like to lead. I can be seen at the top of my game and nothing gives me greater satisfaction and energy than somebody recognising something I've done well or achieved. I think because I want to be successful, I create my own success and energy. Hard work, focus and having a good team around me that I am comfortable will deliver what's needed in the business, all those elements energise me.

Thomas Martin also mentions working hard as generating energy:

"I try and do the right thing for people to the very best of my ability, and don't cruise around. Right now the economy is in a recession, and yet we're flying; I've never worked harder. You could say that we should be exhausted and we shouldn't be doing half the stuff we're doing. But we're taking market share, and that's just so exciting. I'm energised by it."

Peter Pastides has a zest for living life in the moment:

"I have a natural energy for life and curiosity about the world. I am thinking, I can show my children how to never give up on life and that life is there to be lived. Nobody knows about an afterlife. So I want to be doing whatever I am doing right now because this to me is paradise now, and you need to hit that with with full force, without burning yourself out. Life's a party; this is the party."

His curiosity coupled with energy fires his innovation:

"I am always looking for ways to improve things. Nothing is ever 100%, that's the beautiful world that we're in. I can apply software, process and technology to improve things, so I think another key part of energy for me is that I am constantly innovating, constantly looking for ways to improve things and building things quickly."

Graeme Powell knows that his enjoyment and energy come from the same source, helping his customers:

"If you are doing something you enjoy you're more excited about it. So, one of the things that I like doing is talking with our customers, understanding what they're trying to achieve and what their financial constraints are and then mentally structuring a deal where they get what they need, and that we do well out of. Quickly working something out where the deal is good for the customer and good for us."

Interestingly, **Elaine Waller** refers to the different forms of energy when she describes her own techniques for energy management:

" I have created lots of practical tools around the mental, spiritual, and physical energies and how to keep those in tune. You can work on spiritual with a small 's, call it your spirit centre, or whatever you like, and practise keeping that stimulated and balanced. This is important and we often forget about it or neglect it. So whatever you want to call your inner self, you need to think how you keep that alive, aware, present and stimulated. Spiritual energy needs feeding.

If you keep your mental energy stimulated positively, avoiding stress that takes you on a downward spiral, you keep your intellect fresh.

Physical energy comes down to healthy eating, exercise, and water. If you keep these three energies in balance on any given day you can observe where your lack of resilience is. Then you can tune up each of them like spinning plates, maybe finding that one or two are out of sync and you can have quick day-to-day checks, which help you put them back in place. For example you can learn to work with your emotions; observe the emotion, name it, hold it, and then pass through it; moving back into a place of balance."

Energy in action: Ian and Chris

Ian gets his energy from three areas:

- Doing new things and taking risks – running events or campaigns that others wouldn't risk
- His sport – he is passionate about his sailing and windsurfing and puts energy into these activities and derives energy from them
- Being fit – he runs at lunch time once or twice a week and plays tennis competitively

As we've already noted, Chris recognises that he is an extrovert in the Myers-Briggs sense, and that he is energised by being with and interacting with other people. He sparks off others, and enjoys bouncing ideas around with them and then taking the ideas to new levels. But he also knows that to recharge his batteries, he sometimes needs his own space, time and quietness. If he notices that his energy levels have dipped, he'll change the pace of his activity, get up and move around, or just do something else for a while to change his mood and state; similar techniques to working with a group of people as a trainer or facilitator, and managing the energy levels in the room.

He says that the excitement of winning, maybe closing a sales deal, is an obvious boost to his energy. And he's also noticed that the achievement of much smaller milestones on the path to a bigger goal, such as implementing some new software, or even buying some new equipment, can give him a significant energy injection.

References

'*Managing your energy, not your time*' Schwartz and McCarthy, Harvard Business Review, 2007

'*Energy is real – A practical guide for managing personal energy in daily life*' Gail Christel Behrend and Claudette Anna Bouchard, human energetic press, 2009

Myers Briggs Type Indicator Katharine Cook Briggs and Isabel Briggs Myers, 1962

Chapter 8 – Authenticity

Be true to you

Achieving your purpose in life requires the honesty to define your own authenticity - that is, know who you are and what you want

Introduction

The clarity of who you are, what you stand for and where you are going is driven by your authenticity. The A for authenticity is the central letter in HEART and is also at the centre of becoming successful.

All the business leaders interviewed could clearly articulate their values and what they stood for with absolute clarity. The Himalayan journey was driven by the authenticity of Ian and Chris, and the academic evidence demonstrates the importance of authenticity in developing trust with those around you.

In this chapter we give an overview of how authenticity was important to the Indian adventure, how to define your own trust and the importance of emotional intelligence in being able to interact in a truly authentic way.

Authenticity in India

In Chapter 3 we heard how Ian asked the holy man: 'What is the meaning of life and why are we here?' Ian's core value of curiosity and his desire for continual learning made him ask the question that gave rise to such a profound answer.

Ian and Chris's fun-loving values and the energy brought on by their belief in the significance of the journey further cemented the sense of common purpose and community on the journey, making the challenges easier to overcome.

Ankur's authentic behaviour was evident to Ian and Chris from the moment they met him and allowed trust to develop very quickly. When Ankur suggested they refrain from sampling the tempting streetfoods available, with their wonderful aromas and colours, they took his advice. They knew it was because he wanted to ensure they both ate 'safe' food.

Authenticity for you - practical guidance

Authenticity comes from reflection and coaching.

Be an authenticity-spotter

Think about authenticity, what it means to be authentic and how it comes across to those around us. What does authenticity mean to you?

Consider someone you know whom you consider to be truly authentic in the way they behave. What do they do to make them a truly authentic person?

- What authentic behaviour have you seen recently?
  - o How did it make you feel?
- What examples of unauthentic behaviour have you seen?
  - o What impact did this have on you?
- What actions have you ever taken that felt 'unauthentic'?
  - o What caused you to act and behave that way?

"To thine own self be true, and it must follow, as the night the day, thou canst not be false to any man." William Shakespeare, *Hamlet*

Authentic living is based on three things:

1. Your experiences and upbringing
2. Being true to yourself and living in accordance with your values and beliefs
3. The extent to which you accept the influence of other people and the belief that you have to conform to the expectations of others

Being authentic is about having your own set of values and standards and living them. But finding your voice and finding your unique way of expressing yourself isn't easy. It's something that every artist understands and knows is most definitely not a matter of technique. It's a matter of time and a matter of searching: soul searching. The same is true of successful business people: it's useful to read, observe and imitate the practices of leaders you admire, and it's about being clear on what is important and what matters to you.

Writing in 'Winning', Jack Welch says the first characteristic of hiring for the top is authenticity. "What makes leaders likeable, for lack of a better word - their realness comes across in the way they communicate and reach people on an emotional level. Their words move them, their message touches something inside... leaders can't have an iota of fakeness. They have to know themselves, so that they can be straight with the world, energise followers and lead with the authority born of authenticity."

"Authentic leadership requires some self-knowledge, not years of therapy" say Goffee and Jones. "You need to determine what is special about you that works with others. What core values fuel you? How have your origins shaped you? What strengths differentiate you? What weaknesses demonstrate that you need others? Then using your understanding of your followers and the particular situations you encounter, determines which parts of yourself to disclose to strengthen your relationships and to inspire others. The key is 'enough'. A bit of mystery keeps you interesting."

Define your values

A value is, simply, something that is fundamentally desirable. When you are identifying your personal values, ask yourself "is this fundamentally desirable to me?"

Look at the list below to help you decide what are your top four values and of course you can add additional values:

achievement   knowledge   promotion

leadership	adventure	location
affection	loyalty	arts
variety	money	challenging
meaningful work	competence	problems
competition	co-operations	sense of community
creativity	decisiveness	honesty
efficiency	expertise	personal
fame	excellence	development
religion	status	ecological
self-respect	security	awareness
growth	influencing	excitement
intellectual status	inner harmony	quality
working alone	working with others	relationships
involvement	wisdom	serenity
teamwork	discipline	supervising others
leading	independence	wealth
mentoring others	recognition	working under
balance in life	open-mindedness	pressure
being a specialist	health	pride
new learning	the right image	tolerance
financial reward	having many skills	financial
solving problems		competence
		meeting
		commitments

Once you think you have identified your values, consider:

- What are the behaviours you exhibit as a result of these values?
- How are you perceived by other people?
- Are these values useful to your development and success?

In their book 'The Leadership Challenge' Kouzes and Posner suggest you should consider the following questions to frame your values:

Chapter 8 Authenticity

- "What do you stand for? Why?
- What do you believe in? Why?
- What are you discontent about? Why?
- What brings you suffering? Why?
- What makes you weep and wail? Why?
- What makes you jump for joy? Why?
- What are you passionate about? Why?
- What keeps you awake at night? Why?
- What's grabbed hold and won't let go? Why?
- What do you want from your life? Why?
- Just what do you really care about? Why?"

Develop your emotional intelligence

It's one thing to have a fully developed set of authentic values, it's another to have the interactive skills to be successful.

Emotional Intelligence is the ability to identify and understand our own emotional reactions and those of others in order to make good decisions and to behave effectively. It's also the basis for personal qualities like self-confidence, integrity, knowledge of our strengths and weaknesses, resilience during adversity, self-motivation, perseverance and our ability to get on with others. People think Emotional Intelligence is about social skills. This idea is part of it, but mostly Emotional Intelligence is concerned with our internal world of reflection. Our internal world drives how we interact and respond to the external world.

One definition of Emotional Intelligence is:

"The ability to monitor one's own and others feelings and emotions, to discriminate among them, and use this information to guide one's thinking and actions." Mayer and Salovey.

It is interesting to observe that some people with obviously good brains seem to falter in life, while others, who appear to have little obvious intellectual ability, seem to do very well.

'Hard skills' are easy to measure and have a strong commercial value. 'Soft skills' or, as we like to describe them, 'core skills' are not so quantifiable though they are equally sought after by employers.

Emotional Intelligence was first described by Edward Thorndike in the 1930's as 'social intelligence', the ability to get on with other people. Keith Beasley used the term 'Emotional Quotient' in Mensa magazine in 1987. Peter Salovey and John Mayer published their landmark article *'Emotional Intelligence'* shortly after and in 1995 Daniel Goleman published his book: *'Emotional Intelligence: why it can matter more than IQ'*.

It was Daniel Goleman who identified five competencies of Emotional Intelligence. He recognised that Emotional Intelligence by itself is not a strong indicator of work performance but rather that it provides the foundation for competencies that do indicate work performance, which are:

Self Awareness	knowing what you are feeling and why
Self-regulation	able to control your emotions, even when circumstances are difficult

Chapter 8 Authenticity

Motivation	able to persist in the face of discouragement
Empathy	able to read and identify emotions in others
Social skills	able to get along with others and handling emotions

He wrote "*IQ offers little to explain the different destinies of people with roughly equal promises, schooling and opportunity.*"

It is important to recognise IQ and Emotional Intelligence are not competing qualities. IQ matters but without Emotional Intelligence, cognitive abilities suffer. For example, good communication involves cognitive ability and emotional capacities such as gauging reactions or presenting information in a way that has the desired emotional impact, especially in sales and marketing situations in business. If you do not get the emotional piece right, then you are not communicating as effectively as you could be.

A research study carried out in the 1950's on PhD graduate students at Berkeley University showed that forty years later (when in their early seventies), their social and emotional abilities were four times more important than IQ in determining their professional success and prestige - Feist and Barron.

A good starting point in developing Emotional Intelligence is to consider your emotional competence. There are plenty of great books on this subject and it is certainly worth reading more into this. As an immediate starting point, consider your awareness of your emotional state.

What emotions are you experiencing right now? On a scale of 1-10, how would you rate each one? It is important to understand where you are at a given point, especially for example, before going into an important meeting. Also, notice there are a number of emotions at different levels.

Next we need to develop our skill of discerning someone else's emotion. Look at someone and can you deduce from their expression, what is their emotional state? Whilst we recognise someone who is obviously happy or sad, it's important to calibrate and recognise people's emotional state. This allows you to relate to a person. Think about what you are seeing and listen to their words as well as their tone and speed of delivery. We do this all the time when we meet people. The trick here is to become aware of doing it so you can develop your ability even further.

Finally, knowing where you are and assessing where the other person is, emotionally, means you create better empathy with them by 'stepping into their shoes'. By aligning your emotions closer to theirs, you build rapport and empathy whilst maintaining your authenticity.

Authenticity and Trust

Trust is a very important element in business decision-making and your authenticity will have an important part to play in this. Being trustworthy is important to success in any career. A model developed by Maister, Green and Galford is a useful tool for considering the elements of trust, and how you can develop the trust you have with others.

The model shows, that for an individual:

$$T = \frac{C + R + I}{S}$$

T = Trustworthiness
C = Credibility (Can they do what they say they do?)
R = Reliability (Will they do what they say they will?)
I = Intimacy (Do I feel comfortable with them?)
S = Self orientation (Do they care beyond their own interests?)

'The Trusted Advisor' Maister, Green and Galford.

The model shows four important elements that comprise trust: credibility, reliability, intimacy, self-orientation.

Achieving trust is about being able to do well across all four attributes, rating high on those above the line, and low on self-orientation. You can build trust by scoring well in two of these elements and lacking slightly in the others, though such people often wonder why they are not as successful as they could be.

Being **credible** within your role is not just about being an expert in a subject; it is about your presence, with a focus on appearance and reaction. Maister, Green and Galford give the example of the credibility of a medical doctor. Their certificate to practise represents their competence, and appeals to both our emotional and rational sides.

Reliability is based on how dependable you are and how much you can be trusted to behave in a particular way. For some people this relates to how often you interact with them. Reliability is based around action. In order to be reliable you need to be able to link words, thoughts, and intention and take action. To score well in reliability, you need to be able to make a promise and deliver, *and* be consistent in doing so.

Being **intimate** is another key element in gaining trust. People trust those who can share intimate thoughts as well as those who show that they care (low self-orientation). Business is personal, both internally with colleagues and externally with customers. Being intimate in business is about showing your "human" side, sharing thoughts and feelings in open discussions, at the same time as demonstrating care and compassion in your interactions.

We become comfortable knowing how credible and reliable we are and can keep a balanced level of **self-orientation** by showing that we care enough to listen to someone. Remember, in the model, the optimum score for self-orientation is a low value.

It is difficult to work with someone who is more into him or herself than caring about others. To develop and maintain a low self-orientation, your conversation should revolve around the other person, offering open-ended questions, without interruption. Focus on defining problems as you have a discussion, without guessing the solution straight away.

To manage low self-orientation, you need to be a friend. Approach customers and colleagues as if they are a friend. If you want to be successful you also need to allow people to feel they can approach you and openly discuss worries and troubles.

Overall, a focus on these four elements, demonstrating them throughout your work is one of the keys to developing trust and being successful. Without trust from others, there is no basis to create a relationship.

Authenticity in action

Thomas Martin finds that his own values are embedded in his company, and he sets great store by honesty:

"My values are reflected in the company's DNA. I do work hard. I do care passionately about the men and women that have chosen to work with us. It's about hard work, integrity, and trying to get it right. It's the humility of when you've got it wrong actually being able to say: OK, I'm really sorry that was the outcome of my actions. I have learned to do that more especially over the last two or three years. It wasn't a natural suit, but I found a way to have that within my DNA. I think in the best businesses no one can claim to get it right all the time but actually the best businesses and leaders show their true colours when they get it wrong: they mend it pretty quickly and they actually get remembered for the solution."

He continues:

"Do what it says on the tin. Don't be found out. Don't be shallow. If you set out to do something, and you're trying to lead an organisation in a certain way, walk the talk. Don't pretend. Don't insult other people by saying one thing and doing another. That is really the key for us as a business: to have the leaders of the business, the senior management team, and all the layers of management underneath actually getting aligned to do what we say we're going to do."

Laurie Young believes his success comes from:

"Honesty and integrity, and being seen as Mr Nice Guy has worked fine for me. I loathe bullies for instance. I notice that most who get to senior levels eventually get fired because their people are scared to tell them the truth. Sometimes being decent and helpful means you get taken advantage of but I think it comes back to you in the end. I notice that the majority of really accomplished people are approachable and decent. One other authentic value that you must not take for granted is sheer hard work. Most successful people are driven and simply get more done than the average person."

Steve O'Hanlon echoes his view:

"I think we should all be big enough to recognise our own mistakes, and to be fair and thoughtful in the way we treat other people. Overall I think if I'm perceived at the end of the day as a fair and thoughtful guy to employees then I am happy with myself."

Graeme Powell also values honesty as a leader:

"If you believe in what you're doing it comes across; if you don't believe in what you're doing then it definitely comes across."

Sir Paul Judge considers the honesty of the organisation:

"I find business to be very honest. In general, business has a terrible image but if there's one that is dishonest, it is soon crowded out and people know about it and other people won't deal with it. In any business interaction, organisation, agency or charity, whatever it is, if there is any sharp practice, word goes around pretty fast, and that organisation doesn't survive. Same for people, you want to be honest, you have to be, there's no point being otherwise, as it's not going to be a long-term solution."

Chapter 8 Authenticity

Honesty is coupled with personal reputation and success for **Paul Hewerdine**:

"Honesty is important: every day you make promises to people, so you have to get on with it and deliver. Your reputation is at stake. And when you do deliver, you should do it really well because you only get one shot at it. You're going to look back in 30 years' time and consider what you've accomplished. In an average life you can do outstanding things if you continue to push yourself."

For **Elaine Waller**, her strong sense of service to others aligns all her values:

" A good starting point is about making a difference. Making a difference to other people, with the energy of commitment. My key principle is being 'in service of' and for the greater good. If I follow those fundamental values, then all my other behaviours line up. So it's about being ego-neutral, with a lack of self-interest, being committed to others, and being committed to what you do. Another important value is having fun."

The fun and enjoyment elements emerge strongly from a number of the conversations. **Graeme Powell** confesses:

"If you're not enjoying it there's no point, you better find something else. Ideally I would have loved to play hockey or cricket for a living but I wasn't good enough. So, I had to find something else that I enjoyed and yes, this is enjoyable for me. I like it. It's really important for me to enjoy what I am doing and to like the people I am working with".

He continues:

"My family laugh at me because when we drive somewhere I point out, that's one of our hotels. I identify with our customers. I think there's passion with most of the people in the company that would be the same. They enjoy what they're doing. Now yes, you need to have the right product, you need to find a price that is appropriate, in order to give the customer good service. All that is necessary but it can be done functionally. If you do it with some excitement and enjoyment and desire it comes across and people really do believe it."

"We did have a recruitment agency say to us, we have never had someone go to your company for an interview and not want to join, why is that? My answer is that it's because we are genuinely excited about the opportunity we have to grow, and that comes across."

Peter Pastides talks about the importance of being in tune with your own emotions, and other people's:

"I believe you can only control 30% of your life. So I am very strong about what we do and where we go, and where there's conflict with someone else it is always best to try and find the middle ground, to find the win-win for both parties. If somebody feels hard done by, that is, if you run them down emotionally or put them down that's not the basis of a long term successful relationship. So you try and find the middle ground. The other thing is compassion and empathy. If you're not in tune with your emotions, whether business or personal, I think there is something seriously wrong. If you work with someone who is struggling in their role and needs help or a family member or friend that needs help you should be able to relate and connect emotionally. I think emotional intelligence, and being in tune with people, is far more important these days than anything else."

A strong value for **Philip Oliver** is to create the right environment for people to develop. He recognises the diversity of talent in a group:

"I think it's important to recognise that there is some value in everybody, and within a disparate group it's there in different ways. I've always tried to create an environment where this can emerge, for the benefit of the organisation."

Peter Pastides refers to the spiritual side:

"I believe in making the most of everything, though it doesn't mean I am totally optimistic and crazy. I have times of reflection; you could say I am spiritual at those times. I'm not religious, but I am spiritual, and I just believe in making the most of everything."

Authenticity in Action: Chris

In the mid 1990's, as a salesperson, Chris made the decision not to follow the line of a traditional sales manager but to focus on the values of trust and customer understanding, unlike the typical charismatic and aggressive sales approach of the day.

One IT Director said to him "Chris, you are not the best salesperson I have ever met, but I do believe you are the most honest, and it is for that reason I am making the decision to choose your solution."

He still remembers at the time feeling hurt, and even now as a sales trainer and consultant he thinks back and asks himself "was I not the best salesman?" He knows this is irrelevant, as he still won the deal, and looking at the qualities and attributes of selling in today's market he concludes that trust, based on honesty and customer orientation, and an ability to help solve customer problems, is a key element to building successful long-term relationships.

Authenticity in Action: Ian

In 1992 the IT giant Fujitsu had implemented radical restructuring across the sales force, losing about 50% of the team. Recognising the problem of morale, the Sales and Marketing director said to Ian, "The sales force needs some motivation." It was clear that during this time of tremendous change, a fresh approach was needed, and Ian already had a reputation for doing things differently. Ian recognised who he was, and what the company needed; by being authentic he knew he would be able to deliver an inspiring event, creating value for the organisation and the individuals in the sales team.

Driven by his key values of excitement and a willingness to take risks, Ian arranged a company retreat with a difference, designed to motivate the sales force and assist them through their tough time.

As the salespeople arrived at the retreat, they found themselves with Olympic athlete and gold medal winner Chris Akabusi. He asked individuals to stand on a chair and speak about why they were successful and then had everyone else shout and applaud and then share how it had made them feel.

After a while the team went outside, met by someone who looked like a Hell's Angel and built like a brick house. He looked at them and said, "Tonight, you are going to have some fun. You are going to do a fire-walk."

They took an hour to practise and prepare and then moved to the door to be confronted with two lines of burning embers. Everyone walked on the coals and participated. Everyone cheered afterwards.

The next day, after watching the video and sharing his Olympic victory with Chris they all felt fantastic and left ready to go out and win more business.

Applying authenticity to the event had worked. The director remarked that anyone else would have organised an event along traditional lines, but he had asked Ian to lead the project because he knew he would get something highly original. Ian's belief in the activity, and driving it through with passion, made it a success.

References

'*Hamlet*' William Shakespeare, 1603

'*Winning*' Jack Welch, 2005

'*Why Should Anyone be Led by You?*' Rob Goffee and Gareth Jones, 2006

'*The Leadership Challenge*' Kouzes and Posner, 2007

'*Emotional Intelligence*' Mayer and Salovy, 1989

'*Emotional Intelligence: Why it can matter more than IQ*' Daniel Goleman, 1995

'Emotional Intelligence and Academic Intelligence in career and life success' Feist and Barron, 1996

'The Trusted Advisor' Maister, Green and Galford, 2002

Chapter 9 – Resilience

Know where you are going

You need to take the knocks and handle the challenges on your journey

Introduction

All the business leaders interviewed have had setbacks in their lives and careers. What sets them apart is an ability to handle these knocks and continue to reach their vision.

A set of strategies to cope with the setbacks you face on the journey to success is an essential part of your toolkit..

Evidence shows that two of the most important factors that drive success are clarity in terms of where you are going and a network of support and resilience.

In this chapter we define *resilience* and demonstrate strategies for building your personal resilience.

Resilience in India

In Chapter 4 we heard that not long after they had started cycling up the mountain road from Chamba to Jot, a 2000 metre climb in the hot afternoon sun that's equivalent to climbing up Mount Snowdon, the tallest mountain in Wales, twice in an afternoon, Chris found himself suffering from an acute pain in his right knee every time he pushed down to pedal. He had no other option but to stop. This was serious, and was threatening Chris's journey altogether. Chris was deeply anxious at the thought that he might not realise his goal, but the very thought of his goal spurred him on.

Chris broke the problem down into components to help him deal with the situation:

- There were some steps that he could take, one at a time: massage the knee; apply Reiki; cycle a little; rest; carry on
- He used his sense of humour, when talking to the local children
- He enjoyed the support of the team around him for encouragement and the eight litres of water he consumed as he cycled up the mountain

Examples of setbacks started at the time of conceiving the journey: the loss of a friend requires resilience in its own right and Ian's desire to undertake a pilgrimage in his honour is a perfect example of setting a goal to guide one through a time of personal challenge.

At other times on the adventure the reservoirs of resilience of both men were called upon: the tediously long car journey from Delhi to Chamba (and back); the 1000 metre climb at the end of the first day; and the climb on foot to the eco hotel at Himalayan Orchards.

So what is resilience?

The occupational psychologist Dr Michael Pearn has described resilience as the ability to stay positive and effective in difficult or challenging circumstances and feel positive about the future. He suggests an integrated life strengthens resilience. The elements of an integrated life are shown in his model below:

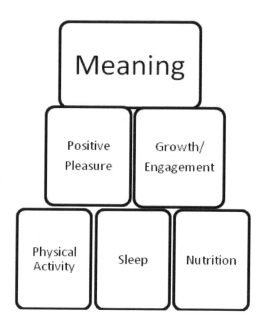

Dr Pearn suggests the foundations of an integrated life are physical activity, sleep and nutrition. The foundation of success according to this book is Health and that also builds on those same three elements.

In Dr Pearn's model, the foundation gives us a positive experience and growth as a human being. Ultimately this gives us meaning. He therefore suggests that having meaning through an integrated life allows you to be resilient to difficult situations. These elements help to reduce anxiety and the effects of stress, making us feel better.

As an example, how often do things look different the next morning compared with how they looked the evening before?

Professor of psychology Dr Barbara Fredrickson advocates ensuring you have positive emotional states to build resilience. These states include joy, gratitude, serenity, interest, hope, pride, amusement, inspiration, awe and love. Positivity means that our pulse rates and blood pressure return to normal more quickly after we feel stressed, and it helps undo the harmful effects of negative emotions such as fear, worry, anxiety and depression.

In her book 'Positivity' Dr Fredrickson says that a simple way to build positivity is to ensure you maintain a ratio of 3 to 1 or higher of positive to negative emotion. As you develop positivity, so you achieve good mental habits that support your resilience.

Resilience for you - practical guidance

More and more companies are downsizing and re-organising in response to the contraction of markets and economies. The ever-changing business landscape and the challenges it brings means that resilience is becoming a seminal skill for business managers.

Gill Corkindale has developed a simple 8-point checklist to guide you in developing personal resilience:

1. **Feel in control** – you can't control events but you can control the way you interpret and react to them
2. **Create a personal vision** – set some realistic goals and take regular steps towards achieving them. Ask yourself 'what is the one thing I can achieve today?' rather than focus on the overarching goal
3. **Be flexible** - accept that change is part of life and that you will have to adapt to changing circumstances
4. **Get organised** – don't react to everything as it happens, organise your day and time so that you can move towards your goals
5. **Be able to solve problems** – work on your problem-solving techniques. Work with coaches and learn different models to interpret what is happening to you
6. **Be socially competent** – develop your emotional intelligence as it will help you to understand what those around you are really saying. Courses in body language and Neuro Linguistic Programming are good starting points
7. **Get connected** – develop your social and business networks. How many LinkedIn connections do you have and how are you using social media to communicate your position and move forward?
8. **Be proactive** –don't wait for events to have an impact on you; take charge and influence the way they turn out

As a line manager, if you create, develop and manage a resilient team, you are helping the individuals become resilient, and that will benefit all those who work with them.

Help individuals to understand the team goals. Enable goal-setting for the team so that every member of the team feels they have contributed to the overall team goals, and they can see their own goals in the context of the team goals

Create an environment for mutual support. A well-structured team, where there is mutual support and coaching, operates at a higher level than one where members come to work just to do the job. The more time you invest in creating that feeling of common purpose the greater the resilience of the team

Communicate. Make sure that everyone in the team understands what's happening, how the team is performing and what the challenges are. The more effort that is spent on keeping team members briefed the greater their ability to internalise the necessary actions and respond as needed

Be human. People want to be led and work with human beings. For the vast majority of people the task is just one aspect of the role; they seek social interaction too. The team leader has an important role in ensuring that this facet of team dynamics is in place. At times, when the going gets tough, people are more inclined to help their friends than anyone else

Praise. People want to be part of a winning team, so make sure you accentuate the highs and deal with the lows sensitively

Dealing with setbacks in teams

Writing in *'Three ways to turn setbacks into progress'* Teresa Amabile and Steve Kramer set out a three point plan for dealing with setbacks. They argue that rarely does a team complete a project without some sort of setback, so it is critical that managers keep people engaged, productive and focused when things go wrong. Here are the ways to do that:

Reframe. Don't treat setbacks as failures and don't assign blame. Instead, frame them as learning opportunities and focus your team on solving problems not wallowing in them.

Don't constrain the solution. When faced with a problem, you don't always have to figure out the solution right away. Be open to changing direction and give people the freedom to look for alternative answers.

Focus on small wins. Help people to see their progress in other areas. If people have regular successes, even small ones, then a setback will sting less.

It's in your head

Writing in *'The Resilience Factor'*, Reivich and Shatte suggest that to deal with challenges you need to understand the way in which your mind works. In particular they focus on the idea that a person's first response to handling adversity is usually based on facts that don't exist or internal conversations that are not rational. Their advice falls into the following areas:

Learning the ABC – understand how your beliefs affect your feelings and behaviour

Avoiding thinking traps – when things go wrong do you jump to conclusions, always blame yourself; assume that you know what another person is thinking?

Detecting icebergs – these are the deeply held beliefs about how people and their work should operate and who they are and want to be. They are called icebergs because they often sit below the surface and describe how we want to live and can explain apparently irrational outbursts or reactions

Challenging beliefs – a key component of resilience is problem solving. How effective are you at solving the problems you encounter day to day? Thinking styles can often cause people to misinterpret problems

Putting it in perspective – don't waste valuable time and energy worrying and putting yourself into a state of paralysis about events that have not even happened

Calming and focusing – people can be overcome by stress and their emotions can come on so quickly that they can't think straight. Techniques to ground and handle these are an essential part of any manager's kit bag

Real-time resilience – a skill whereby you can quickly move from negative to positive thoughts

Resilience in action

Business leaders have had to draw on their resilience many times over the course of their careers, and to bounce back to success. Each of them has a good understanding of how they manage to do that.

For **Elaine Waller**, it's about self-knowledge:

"The most important thing is to 'Know Thyself'. I believe that the more you understand who you are, how you operate, and what your triggers are, the more you can observe yourself and capture the negative thoughts and feelings before they become behaviour. You can then work with day-to-day practical tools that help you come back to a place of balance. That's what keeps me resilient."

Analysis features strongly, in terms of learning from what has happened, and dealing with it. **Graeme Powell** says:

"When things don't work out, maybe you don't win a deal, I think you do take it personally. You think what could I have done differently? You review it as a corporate entity, what could we have done differently? I think the key to bouncing back from that is either being able to answer there's nothing that we could have done better, or to learn for next time, then apply it and move on."

He continues, applying this to his team:

"I believe in the maxim that good people learn from their mistakes, poor people fail to learn from their mistakes and great people learn from other people's mistakes. Following this logic, a person making a mistake is not necessarily as big a problem as some people might try and make out. The key is to ensure that they can and do learn from their mistakes."

Fergal Morris works with a mentor to analyse the situation:

"In a career of 30 years I have had a few setbacks. The important thing is not to have a knee-jerk reaction. I take time to gather my thoughts and fully understand the reason for the setback and learn from it. I always let the emotions calm down first, so depending on the type of setback it could be an hour or two, or weeks, or even months to get full clarity on the issues. I have always tried to find time to really think it through and then find somebody that I can work with as a mentor to discuss what happened, the reasons why it happened and what I would do differently with hindsight. And then I try to bring that learning forward."

Analysis combined with a positive attitude works for **Paul Hewerdine**:

"I think overall I have a very positive outlook on life in that I don't really take knockbacks to heart. I've always been good at rationalising, so when something happens that appears to be a setback, I don't take it personally, but I think around it and rationalise as to why it happened."

Similarly, **Peter Pastides** draws upon his core values, as a realistic optimist:

"'Optimistic reality' is that I believe I can do anything but within the constraints of reality. And the difference between success and failure is in someone who understands about realism, so when you get into something you have to work out very quickly if it's going to materialise into anything, any good. It's soul-destroying if you continue to try to do something that is never going to work, so I think optimistic reality is important. Determination and flexibility are the two other things that I

think are key, alongside emotional intelligence, that is, being able to tune in and deliver. But you have to be determined. There have been many times where I would have liked to have folded up and gone into a dark hole and forgotten about life's responsibility, but I didn't."

He is clear on the technique he uses for analysis:

"I have a mental process that I go through, anytime I'm faced with a major problem. I look for three solutions immediately. And with setbacks, whether personal or in business, it's the same: I immediately look for three things. I look for a comforting place to go and I look for the worst case and the best case. I evaluate those. You don't push yourself so hard you'll have a breakdown and kill people and yourself, and you don't make bad decisions that put you in your worst place. So that's how I deal with the ups and downs."

Setbacks are opportunities for **Steve O'Hanlon**:

"I see setbacks as opportunities to over achieve. My setbacks are merely the roadblocks that are put in the way that sometimes force you to make a choice, take a different path, alter your behaviour, or alter the pattern that you're working on. That can work out to your advantage.

"I would say I've learnt how to deal will the word "no" an awful lot and I never look at any setback as something that is a problem. I look at it as an opportunity to grow, and I think about how I am going to get to the next level and that's why I have advanced in my career."

Laurie Young has a simple take on resilience:

"I'm very determined. I say to my sons that falling down is not the issue, it's how you get up that matters. You will make mistakes and life will give you a kicking from time to time but its the bloody-minded sloggers that keep getting up who get somewhere."

He goes on to give an example of how a potential disadvantage can be turned to an advantage, based on the general observation that many dyslexic people are better able to stand back and relate to the context of a situation rather than focus on the detail:

"I'm dyslexic and used to be very ashamed of that. When I was at school it was not a recognised difficulty so I used to redo homework again and again. I have now published over a million words in books and articles which are read across the world. My weakness is also my strength because the peculiarities of my own brain allow me to see the big picture, where others don't. Now I don't care who knows."

Sir Paul Judge believes in a strong vision as the way to overcome setbacks:

"If you've got a vision that is really what's driving you. Classic cases, Henry Ford, Honda, IBM, against huge odds they thought they could do a better thing and after years of financial difficulties and all sorts of problems they realised their vision. Now there were no doubt another 100 people equivalent to them, with what they believed to be equally good visions, but they never saw the light of day."

He tempers this with a measure of realism:

"I think I am too resilient, if that's possible. When I get going on a project I really do like to see it through, even though there are a

Chapter 9 Resilience

lot of reasons why it might not be successful. I'm hoping that it will be successful, so I fight setbacks and I possibly even fight them too much so that at some stage you have to cut your losses."

A similar strong focused vision is evident if you look at the business life of Sir Richard Branson; he started his first ventures selling advertising space in his music newspaper from a coin-operated phone box and went on from there to create a brand that covers record labels, airlines, train lines, banks, retail networks and telecommunication companies. His latest venture, Virgin Galactic, is testimony to the fact that almost anything is possible if you have a vision.

When **Chris Stock** set up his own company he had a vision to create a business delivering skills to business managers. The first few years were extremely challenging, so much so that he had to finance the business using loans on his credit cards. *"At one time I had over £100,000 on the cards, yet the clarity of my vision helped me through this period."* Chris used many of the other tools and techniques covered in the theory explained here, including setting up support networks: he used Ian as an informal coach and stayed optimistic by developing techniques to always talk about the progress he had made.

He reflects further:

"There have been a number of challenges, and highs and lows, over the years on the journey to where I am now. My natural style is to be an optimist; I am very positive. I am very clear on the goal, so when sometimes things haven't gone to plan, I see them just as learning opportunities. I have taken those challenges, learned from them and seen them as a way of improving, a way of working more effectively in future."

Ian Hunter talks about how his positive attitude has helped him overcome difficulties:

"I have a simple approach to setbacks: evaluate what needs doing and then get on with it. I know that sometimes the challenges have been in my head, that is, stress or fear of failure. At those times, meditation and sport have helped."

References

'Positivity' Dr Barbara Fredrickson, 2009

'Resilience: How to Build a Personal Strategy for Survival' Gill Corkindale, Harvard Business Review Blog, 2009

'Three ways to turn setbacks into progress' Teresa Amabile and Steve Kramer, Harvard Business Review Blog, 2011

'The Resilience Factor: 7 keys to finding your inner strength and overcoming life's hurdles' Andrew Shatte and Karen Reivich, 2002

Chapter 10 - Team

Unite

You can't do something special by yourself, you need to work with others and learn from others

Introduction

The final part of this book is devoted to the most important area that underpins success: Team. In a team we have the ability to learn from and work with others. We team all the time in our lives, whether it is a virtual team, an organisational team or a task-orientated team.

The ability to be an effective member of these teams (not necessarily as a leader) will determine the outcome of the activity you participate in. The skills needed to be able to unite those around you encompass communication, motivation, and emotional intelligence, and the manner in which you apply your energy, health and resilience to the challenge you operate.

The business leaders we interviewed talk about the importance of people and doing the right thing with those people as essential to their own success. The trip in India would not have been possible without the ability to create empathy and create a team that is focused on the right outcome.

Team in India

Ian and Chris considered the importance of the team in helping them achieve their purpose on the journey in the Himalayas.

The local support team

Their guide, driver and cook were invaluable and the trip would not have been possible without them. Through troubles and setbacks, the team supported them, and gave encouragement with their positive attitude.

Ankur their guide supported them in so many ways. On the first cycling day, when the pair took a dirt track off the main road, which led to a dead end, Ankur called them on the phone to tell them to turn back, as he was watching over them from the car some distance away, to ensure they were on the right track. Throughout the trip he gave them an insight into the local culture, such as etiquette and protocol in temples, as well as the history of British occupation and local history, that enriched their experience. To overcome the language barriers the two Europeans faced in communicating with the many local people they met, Ankur and the team acted as interpreters.

As the dark of the night crept in behind them as they cycled, the car followed providing the pair with light from the headlights leading them to their destination. And when Chris needed to find a mobile phone signal, the driver went out of his way to find one, so that Chris could send a blog back to everyone in the UK who was supporting him.

Dinesh, the cook, provided the two with food, and refreshments to last them their journey. He was at pains to ensure they only ate safe food, so they wouldn't be ill on their journey.

All of them agreed the stopping places to meet with the two cyclists on their journey, and then worked to build campsites. Tents, fire, food and drink were always ready and waiting when they arrived.

Forming the team

Ankur, Dinesh and the driver had not met each other before this trip and quickly had to form a team among themselves to support Ian and Chris. Ankur took charge of leading the support team. However, they had no idea of what the Europeans expected and wanted, as they had not worked with Europeans previously. Similarly, Ian and Chris had not been in such a situation before. This caused communication problems between the team as a whole for the first part of the journey. For example, at the end of the first cycling day, Ankur explained that the two hundred metre ride he had mentioned was missing a thousand metres. He had decided not to reveal the real nature of the ride as he did not want to worry Ian and Chris. At that stage he did not appreciate that Europeans like clear and straightforward information and to know where they stand, whereas in India it seemed to Ian and Chris that people prefer things to unfold more gradually.

The team of two

Ian and Chris had worked together to make this trip possible: by joint planning and providing mutual support they had accomplished this great adventure. Organisation was key in achieving what they both set out to do, involving days and hours of research in guide books and on the internet. But this wasn't just about planning the eight days they would spend in India; they had to ensure they prepared for the adventure appropriately.

They recognised that they were complementary to one another in their styles and approaches. Ian brought structure, planning and creativity to the partnership, and Chris added the extra energy and exuberance to make it happen.

The trip created a good friendship in their team of two. Ian and Chris did not know one another very well before they embarked on this adventure, but in working so closely to realise a common purpose, they each came to understand the other person extremely well. This was in addition to the development of self-knowledge along the way. They shared the realisation that the lessons they were learning were just as applicable in their business lives.

The wider team

They both agreed this journey would not have been possible without support from friends and family: their support in training, and their understanding of the hours away from home were essential. It requires a very tolerant partner to put up with a Himalayan adventure.

The blog was a way of communicating to all the team members who had supported the journey, and who were back in the UK. They were sharing in the experience as it happened, and glad to know from the daily updates that all was well with the cyclists. For that reason it was important to keep the blog up-to-date, as an essential team communication.

What makes a team?

In their book 'The Wisdom of Teams' Katzenbach and Smith have defined a team as a small number of people with complementary skills who are committed to a common purpose, with performance goals and an approach for which they hold themselves mutually accountable. Consider the team or teams of which you are a member. Ask yourself: are you committed to a common purpose, do you have clear performance goals and does each of you hold yourself mutually accountable? And if not, then what can and will you do to fix it?

Belonging is an important concept in a team, and our self-esteem in part springs from it, in turn affecting our performance. Sociologists define the characteristics of belonging as:

- Frequent interaction of the team members
- Free from destructive conflict and negative feelings
- Stable and likely to continue
- Mutual support and concern

Consider: what are you doing to ensure that belonging to your team reflects these characteristics?

High performing teams

Working effectively as a team is essential in today's business environment. Quite simply, a high performing team will be greater than the sum of its parts; the cliché "1 + 1 = 3" is true. A new team cannot be expected to perform to an exceptional standard from the start, but the quicker it can get up to speed, the better. However, a strong foundation is key and the process must not be rushed. It takes patience and professionalism to build the foundation appropriately. When the team becomes high performing the results are worth it, and it can be a fun environment in which to work.

The development of a team usually follows recognisable stages as it grows from a group of people coming together to a high performing team working towards a common purpose. The phrase *'forming, storming, norming and performing'* was coined by psychologist Dr Bruce Tuckman in 1965 to characterise stages of team development, based on his research.

The **forming** stage is when the team has recently come together: members are polite and positive towards one other. Some may be excited about the tasks that lay ahead while others are anxious, and they are unsure how the team will evolve. It is important to determine a leader or chairperson if one isn't assigned. There may be discussions during this stage about how the team will work together. This can prove difficult for those whose inclination is to plunge into the team task. Usually, this stage is short and might last only for the first meeting.

After reality sets in and the team moves into the **storming** phase, the leader's authority might be challenged. This

Chapter 10 Team

happens as others jockey for position and their roles and ways of working are defined. Some might feel overwhelmed by their workload or uncomfortable with the suggested approach, others might resist taking on tasks and question the value of the team goal. Some might feel comfortable with their role but get caught up in the crossfire. This is the point at which some teams fail to meet their purpose. Even those teams who carry out the task might feel they are on an emotional rollercoaster, and they focus more on the job in hand without the support of established processes or relationships with their colleagues; the team is not performing as well as it might.

In time the team shifts into the **norming** stage where a hierarchy is established. Team members come to respect the authority of a leader, and others show leadership in specific areas. Better relationships with colleagues means that members now feel they can ask one another for help and provide constructive criticism in turn. From this, the team develops a stronger commitment towards the common purpose.

Between the storming and norming behaviour there is often an overlap. With new tasks, the team may reflect behaviours associated with the storming stage.

The **performing** stage shows the team is working well and progressing towards the shared vision of their purpose. This stage is supported by agreed processes and structures that have been put in place earlier on. Without affecting the performing culture, individuals join and leave the team. The leader is able to delegate work and can focus on developing individual members of the team.

What can you do?

Your role within the team may or may not be that of the leader. Either way, for you to be really successful requires the support of the team. If you are not the leader, and he or she is doing a great job, how do you support that person for even better results? If the leader is struggling, what can you do to help drive and support the effective development of the team? Your own success is built on the team's success, so being apathetic is not an answer. It is your responsibility to ensure 1 + 1 = 3 (or more!).

Use the Tuckman model

Stage	Activity
Forming	• Establish clear objectives
Storming	• Establish processes and structure • Work to smooth conflict and build good relationships between team members • Remain positive and firm in the face of challenges • Be assertive and ensure conflicts are resolved
Norming	• Help the team take responsibility for progress towards the objective This is a good time to arrange a social or a team-building event
Performing	• As a high performing team, the aim is to have a "light touch" towards one another

Learn to recognise the stages in the *forming, storming, norming and performing* model, and consider how they relate to your own team, to help you influence its development. You will need to vary your approach depending on the stage your team has reached: you need to do the right thing at the right time.

For each of the four stages, there are a number of activities to assist the development of the team.

It is useful to review regularly which stage the team is at, so you can make adjustments as necessary. This will change at the performing stage when a "light touch" approach is required.

Belbin Team Roles

We often start a conversation with a colleague we haven't previously met by asking them what they do and their job title is usually the response. In reality the job title only gives us a clue as to what they do. What would be more useful especially in terms of the team is to understand who they are, and what are their strengths and weaknesses in the workplace.

Dr. Meredith Belbin developed the concept of *Team Roles* to allow people to identify their natural role within the team. She found it was important to have a balance of roles across the team. Too many of one or none of the other would hinder success when looking at a task or project from start to finish.

In the Belbin Team Role model there are nine team roles:

Plant: Highly creative. Good at problem solving.

Monitor Evaluator: Logical. Makes impartial judgements.

Co-ordinator: Objective-focused. Delegates the work.

Resource Investigator: Provides knowledge of competition. Promotes the team's ideas outside the team.

Implementor: Develops and executes a practical plan or strategy.

Completer Finisher: Ensures the task is completed. Ensures highest standards at the very end.

Teamworker: Identifies and completes work to be done throughout. Gels the team.

Shaper: Drives the team forward. Challenges individuals.

Specialist: Has in-depth knowledge in the subject area.

It is important to remember these roles are describing your natural behaviour as opposed to roles assigned to individuals. From the list of nine team roles, which do you recognise in yourself? Which do you recognise in other team members? Is the team balanced? There are more accurate ways to determine team roles and doing this as part of a team-building session can be fun too.

Communicate effectively

Lack of communication is a common reason teams do not perform as well as they might. The method of communication is very significant, and there is more choice with the abundance of electronic communication. You need to think about what you want to communicate, how it is likely to be received, and then choose the best medium. For example, email is useful, but a *complex* message delivered by email is not the best way to get that message across. As the model below shows, this could lead to mistrust and lack of commitment.

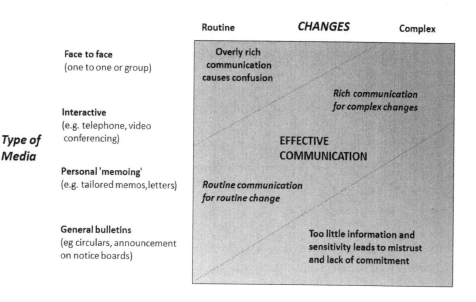

The model is based on one developed by R.H. Lengel and R.L. Daft in 1988 (see references).

Overcome barriers to effective teamwork

Finally, it is worth considering the barriers of effective teamwork to identify which ones may exist within your team. If they do, what do you need to do to eradicate them?

- Lack of clarity about objectives or goals
- No agreement with objectives or goals
- Lack of trust
- Ineffective communication
- Poor development of knowledge, skills and behaviours
- Low motivation
- Poor selection of team members

Teams in action: the business leaders' views

There's a strong awareness of the benefit of different capabilities and viewpoints within a team. **Graeme Powell** puts it like this:

"I make sure I listen to the way other people operate. Within my team we are very different, well, most of us are very different people. Where there is someone whose approach and natural inclination is very similar to mine he or she is the person I listen to the least. I know that sounds weird, but it's because I'm not learning anything. Where somebody has a completely different approach to me, I listen to that person a lot. And what I try to do is to say, OK, their approach is from this angle and I am approaching it from that angle. If we reach the same result, that's brilliant. If we reach different results, then I need to understand why they are thinking what they are thinking. And yes when I am looking to employ people I am looking for someone whom I enjoy working with but no I don't want them to think the same way I do."

Fergal Morris talks about understanding the different strengths in his team:

"If you want to be successful, I think you have to understand teams, and get to know your own team very well. Know the strengths within your team and make sure you use the team strengths when you need them."

With his team, **Paul Hewerdine** considers contribution not just in the current role but the next one:

"We hire people we know have a huge amount of potential and the right attitude, who like us and want to do something and do it really well. But we don't pigeon-hole them, so we might hire them to do one role and then actually think that they have got really good qualities elsewhere and encourage them to move into another role. So I think if you look after people, they grow as a result, and that benefits your business."

Similarly, loyalty and faith in team members is important to **Graeme Powell**. He talks of one of his sales team:

"He said to me, I haven't sold anything for 9 months, I am paid much more than is normal: if I were you I would fire me. I said actually, I think you're doing the right thing. I think you're in a bit of difficulty right now, your market is not strong economically at the moment but I think you're doing the right things, and if you keep doing the right things you will eventually get the right results. A little while later he signed a big deal. Loyalty is important if you believe in people."

Thomas Martin talks about the mutual benefits of a good relationship between leader and team:

"When I think about my career I know I have had the privilege of working with some great people. I have been able to share my enthusiasm and passion for this business with them, so they are thinking about a career and not a job. These brilliant people in turn help me shape my own thinking."

The supportive team leader is characterised by **Philip Oliver**:

"The important thing is to get good people, work with them and help them do their best."

Team in action: Ian and Chris

Chris's story

While at Intel, Chris wanted to formalise his business experience and the knowledge he had gained over his career to date by taking an MBA. He remembered how he felt when he joined the class. He did not have a first degree and had just done 'ok' at college, so he did not perceive himself as particularly academic.

The students were placed into a syndicate group of seven people. This was to be the study group for the duration of the programme.

Their first assignment was a piece of work as a group. Chris remembers working with Catherine. Catherine had a PhD in Chemistry and was an extremely bright person. During their first piece of work together, neither really knew the answer to the question posed. Chris's approach was practical based on his business experience and

Catherine's approach was academic, and between them, they were able to pull together their thinking and come up with the correct approach and answer. Chris realised it took both of them to get it right. As Chris and Catherine worked through their part of the task, the rest of the group carried out work on their sections. The group came together to collate their findings into a single assignment and presentation, which resulted in an A+ for their first piece of work. Chris was of course used to working as part of a team both in IBM and Intel, though experiencing it within this environment had a big impact on him. This was the start of their journey as a team.

In the early stages of creating the team, they agreed on a set of values and objectives to adhere to. Though they had joined the MBA as individuals, the team became very important to their definition of success. They agreed that success for them was everybody completing the MBA and achieving a Master's degree. Having such a shared objective as a foundation ensured they all supported each other, whilst still appreciating that the Master's degree was an individual qualification.

The team was high-performing. It was a lot of fun and the work they produced, both individually and collectively, was of an extremely high quality.

Ian's story

Ian was well aware of the team effort involved in getting him to the European Elvis Singing championships a couple of years ago. His determination was coupled with the patient perseverance of his singing teacher, and friends and family who tolerated (or supported) him practising at home and attended many of his rehearsals. Those same people even came to the event itself to cheer him on. Everyone had a role to play, and though Ian was the performer on stage soaking up the applause, it was truly a team effort.

References

'*The Wisdom of Teams: creating the high performance organization*' Jon Katzenbach and Douglas Smith, 2003

'*Tuckman's Group Development Model*' from the paper '*Developmental Sequences in Small Groups*' Dr Bruce Tuckman, the *Psychological Bulletin*, 1965

'*The Selection of Communication Media as an Effective Skill*' R.H. Lengel and R.L Daft, *The Academy of Management Executive, 1988*

About the business leaders interviewed for this book

Paul Hewerdine

Paul is co-founder and Director at Earnest, one of the fastest growing and most successful B2B marketing agencies in UK. Within just two years, Earnest agency has launched, had instant market success, and now it's just won the hugely coveted B2B Marketing Agency of the Year award. In short, Paul and his partners have taken the B2B agency world by storm. Paul started out at Hitachi, and then moved to the agency world in 1995. He spent ten years at the agency Wilson Harvey, before moving to Loewy, one of Europe's fastest growing brand communications agencies, where he headed up the B2B team. Now at Earnest, he is working with heavyweight clients such as Cisco, Fujitsu and Vodafone.

Sir Paul Judge

Sir Paul is a prominent international businessman and philanthropist who founded the Judge Business School at the University of Cambridge. He started his career with Cadbury Schweppes where he led a management buyout of the food business to form Premier Brands in 1989. He moved into the public and political sector and was appointed Chairman of Food from Britain which led to his being voted the 1992 Food Industry Personality of the Year. He became a Ministerial Advisor to the UK government in the 1990s, responsible for policy on deregulation, privatisation and competitiveness. Currently he holds a number of international directorships and is widely involved in educational support activities.

Thomas Martin

Thomas Martin is the joint Managing Director of Arco, the UK's leading safety company and a fourth generation, family-owned business, headquartered in the city of Hull in the UK. After several years in London working in advertising and direct marketing, Thomas joined Arco in 1988, and gained experience through telesales, product management, purchasing and branch operations at various seniority levels before being appointed Supply Chain Director and then Joint Managing Director. Thomas upholds the family values that are at the core of Arco and is actively involved in fund-raising for the RNLI and contributing to the local business community through his involvement with the Yorkshire & Humber CBI Council, and he is on the advisory boards of Hull Bondholders and For Entrepreneurs Only.

Fergal Morris

Fergal Morris joined 3M in 1982 in finance before moving into a variety of sales and marketing roles, eventually leading to Managing Director for 3M in Ireland. He completed his MBA at the Smurfit Business School at University College Dublin in 2007 before he moved to the UK, where he further developed his career and ultimately was appointed General Manager 3M Safety Solutions. This role means that he is involved in all aspects of the business from innovation through to commercialisation, and it has

129

given him the opportunity to be involved in two major local acquisitions leading to their integration into 3M. He is a board member of the British Safety Industry Federation (BSIF), as Company Secretary.

Steve O'Hanlon

As President and Chief Operating Officer of Numerix LLC, Steve O'Hanlon leads the company's global operations, from his headquarters in New York, USA. Numerix is the leading independent analytics provider for derivatives and structured financial products, working with more than 400 financial institutions and 45 partners across 25 countries. Steve is the chief architect of the company's sales, marketing, distribution and corporate strategy, which has resulted in unprecedented growth during the last three years. He has more than twenty-five years' experience building emerging market start-up software companies and has contributed to three successful IPO's. He started his career in sales executive positions at Avant–Garde Computing and Nixdorf Computers.

Philip Oliver

Until he recently retired from Fujitsu, Philip was the Executive Vice President Marketing of Fujitsu's Global Business Group, responsible for both strategic input to the chief executive and for all aspects of marketing outside of the domestic market in Japan. He joined Fujitsu in 2004, having spent 25 years in the other global IT giant, IBM. At IBM he moved through a variety of marketing roles, to reach the level of Vice President Worldwide Strategy for IBM Global services. Before IBM Philip was a senior manager at British Telecom. Until 2009 he served as a non executive Director of the UK Crown Prosecution Service.

Peter Pastides

Peter is co-founder of Continuous Insight, a company that provides global customer insight for business-to-business blue chip technology companies. Before that, he held a variety of senior roles in Sales and Marketing, and Business Development, for a number of IT companies located in North America and South Africa, as well as the UK. At school he was a very capable middle-distance runner, achieving the Athletics nationals for 800m. Now, in later life, his passion for sport has embraced hockey, and he has qualified as an England Hockey Board coach, training young people and fund-raising to invest in the grass roots of the sport.

Graeme Powell

Graeme Powell has been Managing Director of iBAHN Europe Middle East & Africa (EMEA) since he founded iBAHN EMEA in 2000. iBAHN enables companies in the hospitality, conference, food service and retail industries to deliver High Speed Internet Access and other technologies to their guests via a world-class IP platform in over 50 countries. He has worked in hospitality and related technology industries for 20 years. Prior to that he worked for what is now PriceWaterhouseCoopers where he qualified as a Chartered Accountant. He is also Treasurer of Carey Baptist Church in Reading, UK.

Elaine Waller

Elaine Waller has spent the last 18 years as a Communications Trainer, Behavioural Coach and Business Counsel, helping individuals or teams to reach their goals and succeed. Through her own practical tools and methodologies she works with areas such as authenticity and personal impact; emotional resilience; personal sustainability and self-leadership. Elaine's ego-neutral approach has gained her a reputation as leader in her field globally and her clients read as a who's who of British industry. She has worked across businesses such as PricewaterhouseCoopers, Bank of America, Willis, 3i, IBM, BP, British Gas, Barclays, Ernst & Young, Nationwide, Linklaters, Fujitsu, Janssen-Cilag, Novartis, ABN Amro, Sainsbury's, Lovells, Johnson & Johnson, RAC Group, BT, Vodafone, National Health Service, Nats and the Defence and Military sectors.

Laurie Young

Laurie Young is a businessman who likes to write. During his line career he held senior positions at BT, Unisys and PriceWaterhouseCoopers. He has also founded, bought and sold a company. Yet, as his education includes a postgraduate business diploma and an MBA, his writing combines practical experiences with sound business thinking. He has extensive experience of the marketing of technology companies having, in addition to his line jobs, advised companies like Ericsson, Motorola, Energis, Hitachi Data Systems, Cable and Wireless, Datex Engstrom, Philips and Nokia.

About the authors

Between them, Ian Hunter and Chris Stock have over fifty years of business experience. Both have trail-blazed in their own areas of expertise, sales and marketing, stepping into academia occasionally, and backed up by a wealth of practical experience. Both have worked in the IT industry since its early years, operating in a sector that constantly changes and necessitates new ways of thinking and behaving, and a focus for both of them has been the practical side of optimising the behaviour of teams. They have experience of large corporate organisations, business start-ups and Small-Medium Enterprises, national and international business.

Chris Stock

Chris is a specialist in sales force transformation, and is managing director of FourThirds, a successful sales consulting and sales training organisation with offices in the UK and the US. He is an experienced keynote speaker on how to transform the sales organisation to deliver exceptional performance and increase sales results.

Chris's career, spanning twenty years, includes senior sales leadership positions at Intel and IBM. He has an MBA from Henley Business School, and is an accredited executive coach as well as a certified Neuro Linguistic Programming trainer. He is a visiting tutor for the Chartered Institute of Marketing and Henley Business School.

Outside of work he is an accomplished snow ski and water ski instructor and contributes to the management of local charities.

Ian Hunter

Ian is an experienced marketing director with extensive technical and professional services marketing experience.

His career includes positions, in the UK and Saudi Arabia, at Plessey, NCC, P&P, ICL and Fujitsu. He has managed teams of up to 100 in sales and marketing and created relationship programmes with leading British industrialists. Ian is a fellow of the Chartered Institute of Marketing and holds the Henley certificate in business coaching.

Ian is a PADI diving instructor, windsurfing and sailing enthusiast. In 2009, he entered the European Amateur Elvis impersonation championships in Blackpool, despite not being able to sing.

The business leaders said...

"Chris and Ian have taken the innovative approach of developing management lessons from physical activity which is fascinating, useful and surprisingly relevant."

Graeme Powell, iBAHN

"In Your Heart reaches the parts other management books don't. A welcome recognition that the heart plays as significant a role as the mind in successful leadership."

Paul Hewerdine, Earnest

"I like it a lot. I like the storytelling approach but in particular I like the integration of all the many sources into a coherent whole. The chapter on trust is particularly relevant to many of today's global problems just as much as it is to one's personal life."

Philip Oliver, ex-Fujitsu